MW01229013

The Case

Kayla's Investigation

by

Det. Christopher Anderson

This is a work of non-fiction. Names, characters, places, and events either are the product of the author's imagination or are used fictitiously. Any resemblance to actual persons, living or dead, events, or locales is entirely coincidental. No portion of this book may be reproduced without the author's prior consent.

https://www.crimeandcookiejuice.com/

Copyright© 2023 by Christopher Anderson

First Paperback Edition

All rights reserved.

ISBN: 979-8-218-16181-1

Printed in the United States of America

Investigations are what I do, it's not who I am.

I've always felt my life had a bigger purpose. It was purpose that led me to marry the first girl I fell in love with much too early by most people's standards. It was purpose that drove my career as a cop, and it was purpose that led me to my success within my field. My goal was to step out of the shadows of the legacy left by my mother, also a career cop. To achieve my goal, I not only needed to be a good cop, but I also needed to be regarded as one of the best. But there was a time when I questioned if I had sacrificed too much to attain that goal. It took a murder that involved thoughts of losing my own child to make me realize I was losing what was most important.

Contents

Acknowledgements

Acknowledgements

To the toughest Cop, I know Sgt. Jessica D. Anderson (my mother),

Mom, I want to take a moment to express my deepest gratitude for all that you have done for me throughout my life and my career. You have been my rock and my guiding light, always there to offer love and support no matter what. As a cop, you faced some challenges that some ran away from. You've seen things that most people could never imagine, yet you've remained strong and steadfast, always putting others first. You are indeed the toughest Cop I know, and I'm so proud to call you, my mom. But behind your bravery and strength, what I admire most about you is your unwavering love and guidance. You've always been there to listen, offer advice, and encourage me to pursue my dreams. You've never judged me, no matter what mistakes I've made, and you've always believed in me even when I didn't believe in myself. Thanks to you, I've grown into the man I am today, and I owe so much of my success to your love and support. You have taught me to be strong, stand up for my beliefs, and always be true to myself. So, thank you mom, for everything you've done for me, for being my role model, for being my mentor, and for being my best friend. I'm so grateful to have your love and guidance, and I will always cherish our memories.

With all my love and admiration your son,
Chris

To Robin (Kayla's Mother),

It would be a disservice if I did not acknowledge your strength, courage, and loving spirit during the most troubling time of your life. As a detective, I have seen many cases, but I must say that your resilience has left a profound impression on me. Your unwavering spirit and determination to overcome the obstacles you faced have been truly inspiring. Your determination to seek justice and protect Kayla's legacy is a testament to your character and strength.

Moreover, your loving spirit has touched the hearts of many people, including myself. Despite the unimaginable circumstance you faced, you have continued to show kindness and compassion towards others, which is truly remarkable. I want you to know that your grace never went unnoticed, and I am grateful for the opportunity to have met such a remarkable person. Your strength, courage, and loving spirit are an inspiration to us all.

Thank you for being a shining light in the darkness.

Sincerely,
Detective Chris Anderson

To my Family,

I wanted to take a moment to express my deepest gratitude to each one of you for the unwavering support you have given me throughout my career as a detective. Your love and encouragement have been my rock during some of the most challenging times in my life.

My work as a detective often required me to be away from home for extended periods, and I know this can be difficult for you all. But you have never once complained, and instead have always been there to offer words of comfort and encouragement. Your belief in me has been a constant source of strength, and I cannot thank you enough for that.

To my wife Anitra, thank you for always being my partner in every sense of the word. Your unwavering love and support have been my foundation, and I could not have done this without you by my side. Your strength and patience have carried me through some of the toughest cases, and I am forever grateful for you.

To my children Kiera, Chris Jr., and Kayla, thank you for being my reason to keep pushing forward. You have, and always, bring so much joy and light into my life, and I am constantly inspired by your resilience and courage. It is my prayer that I can be a source of pride and inspiration for you, as you are for me.

As I continue to serve our community, I want you to know that your support means everything to me. I love you all more than words can express, and I am so grateful to call you my children.

With all my love and gratitude,
Dad

Chapter 1

My Background

Being a homicide detective with the Birmingham Police Department was the most challenging experience I have ever had as a cop. In homicide, you're tasked in every case to bring those responsible to justice. You're also responsible for making sure that the right person is prosecuted for their crime. For most of my career, that's what I chose to do. After twenty-two years as a cop with seventeen of those as an investigator- I realized that law enforcement was much more than just a job for me, it is my ministry. And like any ministry some people become so caught up in their work that they forget what's most important. Marriage, family, enjoying life, and the short time that you have on earth.

As a detective, that time usually came from the ones you loved the most - your family.

During my years as a detective my family sacrificed time with me while I chased bad guys. I remember occasions where I suddenly had to leave birthday parties, ball games, and other special moments. Moments that, even as I type, I regret. I distinctly remember a surprise birthday party that Anitra, my wife, planned for me. It was foiled by a murder that kept me away for most of the night. When I finally walked into the house half of the guests were gone, and the "really, Chris, we discussed this," look was plastered on her face the entire night. But what could I do? To me, my detective work was just as important to life as my life at home. I was stopping people who hurt others. Or, trying to bring those people to justice. In my mind, which protected my family and friends. Those people who came to that party could have just as likely been a murder victim as any of the victims I came across on a near daily basis. That was a tough pill to swallow for me. It was my motivation. And yet, how do you try to convince your family of those same convictions? You don't. It's similar to the explanation that if you leave the house to work then work controls your home.

And if you work from home, home controls work. But the way I looked at it was that I had to go to work to protect my home. That is a heavy weight for my shoulders, regardless how broad they were in my early career. During those first seventeen years I was rarely home. And even when I was home, I always felt as though I had something to do or somewhere else to be. Images of the crime scenes I saw in pictures and "real life-still life" never left my mind. Vague and blurry images of perps kept me on a constant high alert. I remember being on "vacation" with my family, and it was never really a vacation. The times when I should be relaxing, I could never get the cases out of my head. Everywhere I turned I was evaluating the person who walked by me. I was squinting to look at a guy on the opposite end of a parking lot of a venue who had even the slightest resemblance to a perp I was looking for. I was always at the ready. Always working. Always.

I felt as if something was drawing me back to work regardless of where I was or what I was doing. During most conversations with Anitra, I'd be in another zone. Most of the time I was lost inside of a case I couldn't figure out. I felt as if my life was a massive puzzle that instead of getting easier with each new piece I put in place, the puzzle only grew and became more complicated. Nights at dinner my wife would want to download her day to her husband. Even though my body was home, my head was still at work. That's how it had been for the past four years of our marriage. After a while, I think she gave up on trying to communicate with someone who wasn't present. Many of our evening meals – when they happened – ended up with Anitra standing up and releasing a huff or irritation and me quickly trying to recall what she'd just said to me. That of course, I couldn't do, considering I wasn't listening in the first place. So, after her many attempts trying to bond with me and rekindle our connection she submersed herself into spending that time with our children.

My kids, on most nights, would do just about anything to get my attention. To them, I was a superhero out to save the world. I honestly thought while I was away and out working, I was actually protecting them. That's what I told myself to keep me going. What if this was one of your daughters or your son? Would you stop here? Isn't there something else you can do? These were the thoughts that drove me to be a better investigator.

The years I spent in the Birmingham P.D. homicide unit were the hardest. In homicide, you take on a relationship with your victim's family like no other position in the detective bureau. It's your duty and responsibility to speak for your victims as a homicide detective. I know this comparison because I was blessed in my career to work in every investigative bureau in my department. Each unit had their satisfying moments, and they also had their challenging ones.

As a burglary detective the satisfaction came when you could recover the valuables of a distraught parent that worked and saved all year to purchase Christmas gifts for their family. I always thought it took some of the lowest scum of the earth to steal someone's Christmas. But every year I'd have at least forty of those cases. I recall November and December of '99. My partner and I had a string of twenty home burglaries. The connection was that each of the homes had children. Which was important because a home with children is more likely to have Christmas presents than a home without. That meant that whoever was breaking into these homes knew the owners. They were surveying the comings and goings. That opens up a whole new level of problems. Were the perps following school busses in the afternoon to see where kids were dropped off? Were they opening mail boxes or evaluating package drop offs? There is a creep factor when you suspect that the thieves are surveying a home. They were spending time watching kids come and go. And that's something that no parent wants to think is happening. In the end it was a group of teenagers. Those teenagers confessed to eleven of the twenty burglaries and my partner and I were certain we could get charges and convictions for the nine remaining. It was a big day when we made the arrests. But the next morning, there were an additional twenty cases in our inbox. It seemed like the case work would never stop. The reality is that it was never ending. And that became frustrating as a detective. How can I make a change, or make a difference if the cases keep rolling in? I quickly learned to just keep pushing forward.

I think it's important to step back and take a moment to explain the difference between burglary and robbery. I've worked in both units and while many people use the words interchangeably, there is a difference. Burglary is a crime against property. Robbery is a crime against people. Someone breaks into your home and steals the television, which is burglary. You get mugged walking down the street, which is robbery. Because people own property and because there are more nuances to the two types of crime people will often become confused and use those terms interchangeably.

One of the foundational beliefs in police work is that "you're there to make a difference." But when you work your ass off for weeks, take a perp into custody, then go back into the office and find your box filled with more cases that kills your momentum. I never wanted to slow down, or allow the circumstances to dictate my passion and drive. So, after years of working in burglary, one incident at the right time gave me the opportunity to transfer to robbery.

While driving to meet a witness on one of my many burglary cases, I see two males driving erratically on the freeway. The car is weaving in and out of traffic and looked as though they may cause an accident. It was an older model GM that was high on the list of being stolen. So, I followed the car until I could get close enough to see the occupants and run the tag. The young men didn't appear drunk nor was the car reported stolen. But what I did notice is they were both wearing gloves in the car.

Now in some circles this may not be strange. But in 95-degree weather, and a car that's easily stolen, to police officers, this spells two things and neither are good. Either they've just stolen the car, and they're attempting to hide prints, or they're about to do something bad. Either way I needed to look into it. I call for backup and I follow them to a shoe store just off the freeway.

I park my unmarked vehicle just out of direct site. I see the young men get out of the vehicle, pull masks over their faces, and run inside the store.

My mind is racing now, if my back-up arrives too early, we will have a hostage situation. Too late and they may shoot everyone inside. My decision was to let them leave out of the store and get more marked cars to take them down.

It was at that moment the men came running from the business, enter the getaway vehicle and drive away. Myself and two marked patrol cars were able to get the suspects stopped and take them into custody. All the money from the business was recovered, no one was injured, and the suspects were arrested.

Shortly afterwards one of the patrol officers brought the victim over to the arrest location. She wanted to meet me and tell me how much she appreciated my service. When she saw me, she broke down into tears and hugged me. She then began to tell me what happened inside the store. The suspects we had in custody held her at gunpoint and made her employees open the register.

She told me that she and her late husband had purchased that business. But since his passing it was hard for her to keep up the day to day. The experience of this robbery was so traumatic that she didn't want to go back to the store. I tried to give her comforting words of encouragement. And not to give up on her and her husband's dream. She nodded her head in agreement and said she'd do everything possible to push through this experience.

That afternoon, most of the upper brass came down to congratulate and thank me for my courage and quick thinking. It felt good that they recognized the arrest. But for me, knowing those guys were going to prison felt even better.

As an officer, whenever you witness or make an arrest such as this you're interviewed by the detectives. During my interview with the detective working the case she was amazed at how I was able to recognize something wasn't right, and then to react in a way that possibly saved lives.

During my interview I explained to the detective that, yes, I have a skill set but when the skill set meets luck, it's an unstoppable force. I had no idea the robbery supervisor and Chief of Police were watching. They all got a good laugh at this young detective's confidence and the following week I was asked to come to robbery as a detective.

Being a robbery detective was challenging, but was a very satisfying position. There's nothing like taking into custody that asshole who violently victimized a family during a case like a carjacking. Working the robbery cases took more thinking and skill than burglary and it also took more time. There would be nights where I'd stay in the office for hours watching videos and comparing photos trying to find the person responsible.

It always pissed me off when I worked cases where an elderly victim was injured while trying to thwart a robber's attack. And it was here in the robbery unit that my career changed course. More specifically, a string of home invasions involving elderly victims introduced me to homicide and changed my career trajectory. Though to be fair to myself and my career I suspected that homicide was where I'd always end up. These elderly home invasions were just the springboard to get there.

I had been in the robbery unit for one year when I was assigned to work on several home invasions. The cases happened over a period of one week. Each home invasion occurred during the late-night hours. And to add to it, the home invasions occurred in an affluent and low-crime part of the city. Why does that matter? It shows that the criminals were after a big score and willing to be aggressive to get that score. Affluent areas are more likely to have cameras and advanced security systems, diligent neighbors, and neighborhood watch programs, and, often have a stronger police presence. This was an established community where many of the residents grew up but were now in their later years. All of the victims were elderly and female. And all of the home invasions occurred within a mile and a half radius. None of the suspects' descriptions given by the victims were consistent, but the method of entry was. Each suspect, assuming at the time that there was multiple, would enter the home by breaking out a window and entering in an obscure part of the home. That also meant that the suspects had a rudimentary knowledge of a home's layout. Sure, that isn't too difficult, but in an investigation, it shows us that the criminal(s) likely had done this before. More than likely they were in the crime database.

Once inside, the perpetrator would overpower and attack the homeowners. After receiving the reports, I visited each victim—some at their homes and another who had been hospitalized. My victims described the attacks in the same manner. The suspect waited until late at night after they were in bed, opened a front window (often hidden by a large tree or a bush), and entered the residence. After making entry, he would then brutally attack people within the home. In most of these cases the intruder was attacking a female resident unable to defend herself. He would bound the victims' hands, legs, and mouths following the attack and then take whatever he wanted. None of them knew or could identify their attacker. He wore the standard ski mask and dark clothing. Nothing really identifiable.

One of the victims among the home invasions stood out from the others. To protect her identity, we will call her Mildred. Mildred was an 82-year-old woman who was just as fiery as she was spunky. I still remember seeing her swollen face and beautiful smile when I introduced myself to her and the fellow church members in her hospital room. She greeted me with a sparky hello and waved for me to come in with her bandaged hand. She was 5'4, 90lbs, with curly silver hair. While talking to her, I learned that she did not have much family, but she was a well-loved member of her church. Mildred explained how she fought her attacker when she heard him entering her window.

She explained, "I socked that son-of-a-bitch in the face, and that is how I hurt my hand. He is lucky I did not get back to my pistol. I would have given him so much lead he'd think he would have thought he was a number two pencil." After getting as many details of the crime as I could, I asked Mildred if she could identify the suspect. "I do not know if I can, but I will try," she said.

After leaving the hospital, I stopped by Mildred's home. My evidence technician was still there collecting evidence. While there, he told me he found several blood spots where the suspect potentially cut himself and left his DNA on the scene. DNA was a new science for us back then, but it was one of the only leads I had in the case. I just needed to find out whom it belonged to. I worked the overnight shift for weeks to find and arrest the person responsible. During that time, the blood was submitted through the FBI's DNA files, but no match could be found. I was shocked actually. A bold and aggressive perp like this? I knew this wasn't this guy's first time breaking and entering homes. I knew that being an aggressive attacker he was likely armed with in the least a knife but more likely also had a gun or another assault weapon. Motivated by the fight in Mildred and how innocent my victims were in these cases; I was not ready to give up. I knew that as long as this guy was out there and breaking into homes that two things would happen. One is that the more homes he broke into the more emboldened he would become. And two, eventually a victim like Mildred would fight back and end up with more than just bruising and swelling. The more attacks, the more likely these investigations would turn from breaking and entering and unlawful detainment to murder so I needed to work fast

Nevertheless, just as sudden as the robberies started, they stopped. Since the crime and murders in Birmingham had skyrocketed, I figured either my suspect had been arrested or killed. After weeks of working and no new cases, I began to compile as much information on suspects arrested since Mildred's case. There were 874 people arrested during that month. I narrowed the suspects down to about 300 through an elimination process and another 250 thru investigative work. That left around fifty potential persons of interest who could have been responsible. Over six months, I interviewed all fifty persons of interest. During that time, I had compiled so much intelligence on the case that I had to purchase a personal file cabinet to keep the information separate yet accessible. For some reason, I knew I would need it, And boy was I right.

After close to two years of investigating the cases, I almost gave up on making an arrest. Until one early morning I learned of a woman who had been found beaten to death inside of her home. The crime scene was near Mildred's home. Homicide detectives were enroute to the scene to investigate the murder. I then went to my captain's office and explained to him the details of the investigation I had been working on for two years. I also explained to him how this new homicide matched my robbery cases. After hearing those details, he ordered me to partner with the lead homicide detective and aid in the investigation.

Arriving on a fresh homicide scene was intimidating as hell. It was not my first scene, but it was my first time working with a homicide detective. The detectives on the scene had already been alerted that I was to be paired with the lead detective. During the drive over I had prepared myself for the hazing, which is customary in police work. As I exit my vehicle, the lead investigator Frank walked over to me and said, "okay, rookie, you ready for this?"

I tried to cover the fear in my voice by saying, "I'm good." I then grabbed a stick of gum, placed it in my mouth, and walked with him toward the murder scene. As we get to the front porch, I notice the front door's window has been shattered, just like some of my victims. I began to take notes when Frank said, "we have not made it to the good part yet." After finishing my notes, I walk to the victim's bedroom. The bedroom is where the murder took place. The room looked like a scene from the worst slasher movie I could think of. You know the kind. Blood spatter like an artist tripping on LSD. From the moment I entered the bedroom we had to watch our step. Each drop of blood was a piece of evidence, a link to the murder. And these drips were my only link to the murderer. The victim's body was still in the bedroom; her eyes were swollen shut, and multiple bones were visibly broken. The murder weapon was the suspects hands, feet, and a table leg from a broken nightstand in the bedroom. There could have been another weapon, but the place was such a mess it would take time to figure it out. Crime scenes aren't like the movies where everything is neatly placed for the detective to find. A knife could've been tossed into a nearby pond. A piano leg could be in a garbage can. A blunt instrument could be half-hazardly washed and placed in a cabinet.

Blood cast-off and spatter layered the walls and ceiling of the room, and the floor was covered with both spatter and blood pooling. As I took notes of the scene, Frank, the lead homicide detective, walked close to me and asked, "what is this I hear you may have a suspect in this case?" Frank is a veteran homicide detective who has spent way too many days downing snacks and not nearly enough days in the gym. Obesity was a hazard of the trade, and why you are more likely to find a captain with a belly than a rookie fresh out of the academy. He was a good detective, but too many years in homicide have made him cold and numb. The only way he would now crack a smile is if you talked about his upcoming retirement in two weeks. I looked at him and replied, "I don't know if you can call my guy's suspects, but it will be interesting information if it relates to this case." I then begin to explain my open robbery case investigation to him. After hearing the details of my case, he says, "well, rookie, I hope you can close this case in two weeks because after that it will be all yours. I have had enough of this, and I am hanging up my gun, belt, and badge." I nodded my head to acknowledge his statement as he walked away. After being on the scene for a few hours and taking notes, I wondered if I was ready for a case such as this.

I have never been a person that ran from a challenge. Nevertheless, my doubt about my abilities began to rise, thinking about working on a murder case. Months prior to this murder, the same Captain Hinton asked me if I was interested in working for him in homicide, and I turned the position down. In doing so, I had broken an unspoken rule in my department, you do not turn down a position in homicide, especially if you have been asked to come over— the reasons why I will talk about later in the book. However, I didn't think I was ready when I was asked, so I turned the offer down. Up until this day, I regretted that decision.

At that moment, I felt Frank's hand hit my shoulder, "hey rookie, lets head to the building to see this suspect information you have." I pause and stare at him for a moment. His use of the term "rookie" was wearing on me. I'd been a police officer and detective for so long that rookie was hardly a way to describe my time on the force. Sure, I was new to the homicide scene, but admittedly it bothered me, despite showing no outward signs that it did. But my pause wasn't for how Frank addressed me. My pause was because he has no idea how much information we needed to sort through. Remember, I bought an entire file cabinet for this case. I say, "Frank, I have almost 300 suspects in this case if we are lucky. I need more time here to sort through this scene." "Suit yourself rookie, I have got some plans this evening. How about we meet in the morning to sort through your information" he said. "Okay, cool," I reply.

I watch as Frank and most other veteran detectives get in their cars and leave. I then hear my name called, "Chris," and I see a familiar face walking toward me. Rob Briscoe, another homicide detective, was still somewhat new to the team. Rob and I had worked together as detectives before his promotion to homicide, and we worked well together. He was young, sharp, and did not mind teaching what he knew. He knew I aspired to work in homicide one day, so I was confident he would be someone I could lean on. He was just as confused as everyone else when I turned the job offer down. Admittedly, I questioned my decision back then as well.

"Hey man," I say as we shake hands. "Dude how did you let them drop a case like this on you," he said.

"What do you mean?" I asked.

"Chris, Frank is retiring in two weeks. Hell, he's not worked since he put in his retirement paperwork, so you'll end up working this case. Plus, this is a who done it case. They are the hardest homicide cases to solve," he said. When the self-doubt began to rear its head again, Rob saw it in my face and said, "you got this." His words were comforting, and just what I needed to hear. "How much more time do you need on the scene?"

"Just a few more minutes, man. I want to go back over to make sure I have gotten enough notes"" I say.

"Cool, I will wait outside, and then we will go to the building to look over the people of interest you have."

I nodded, realizing that my plans to meet with Frank the next morning to go over the same information may not happen. I knew Frank was retiring and suspected that he was attempting to hand the case over to me just a few minutes before. It was a slippery way to bring me into the homicide unit I'd just turned down. And the suspicious side of me wondered if this was a unique ploy to get me to reconsider. Or not reconsider, but involve me so much that there was ambiguity between my role and that of homicide. Either way it was clear that this murder case was moving my career in a new direction. And seemingly quick.

As I walk back through the house, careful not to step in the dried blood and review the pages of notes made for each room, I notice a closet door in the kitchen. The door was open, and a file cabinet inside had been knocked over. The evidence technicians had not processed this area yet. I noticed a red stain on a shirt hanging inside that closet. It could be nothing because the next room was covered with the victim's blood. Alternatively, it could be the entire case. I call for a technician to take the shirt as evidence. He photographs it and places it in a paper evidence bag. I thank him as I walk toward the door. He stops me and says, "Detective, we just found a name on the victim on her identification. It was piled up with some property of hers in a bag. I will test it for prints, but I took a picture of it." he said.

"What is her name," I ask.

"Grace Garner," he replies.

I take down the information and think that I cannot tell if this is her or not, but I need to run it when we get back to the office.

As I walk outside the house, I realize the sun has gone down in the late afternoon. However, guess who is waiting next to my car? It is Rob. He understood you need that extra time at a scene to process things, plus he knew that I would probably end up working on this case and wanted to see it closed. So, we rode back to the building together. Once there, we began to pour through the mounds of people of interest I had gathered. After a few hours of going through the information and running background information on Grace, we decided to start the following day by going back to the scene.

Detectives had already canvased the area, and that canvas turned up nothing. Nevertheless, we had more information, so a follow-up canvas was necessary. Rob says, "I will call Frank and tell him what we are doing, and Captain

Hinton will not mind; he knows Frank will not work this case." So, we pack up and leave the office. It is now close to 10:00 at night, and I check my cell phone and realize I have missed a few calls from Anitra. The messages were the standard fare for our relationship. Just checking in. Dinner almost ready. Are you going to be home for dinner? Then a few passive aggressive statements about me not being home or in contact. Then a last, "Well, I guess I'm going to bed alone... again." Yeah, I'd been through the litany of these messages time and again. And while I wish I had the heart to dismiss them, the truth was that I felt the pain in my chest and the guilt in my mind knowing that I was being pulled in two different directions. I wish I could've treated my entire career with the same carefree aptitude that a homicide detective retiring in two weeks treated their investigations. But I couldn't. Worse is that I knew work was dominant over my home life and that was never a good thing.

At 7:30 the following morning, I was in my office. The local news had caught wind of the murder, and they had reported about it all night. I wanted to make sure I called Mildred, my robbery victim, to tell her I was helping with the case. Since her case, Mildred and I had stayed in contact with each other, and I figured it would be better for her to know I was still working, especially since this was a homicide. After reassuring her that all our workforce would be shifting to this case, she felt a little at ease.

Rob was there also, so we went back to Grace's home when I hung up. On the way there, I mentally reviewed the crime scene. As we arrived, I noticed something about the house that I had missed the day before. Grace was a 94-year-old woman, she lived alone, and she had no family that we could find. Nevertheless, her yard had been cut, and very recently at that. As Rob exits the car, I say, "I think we need to find the person that cut her grass as soon as possible."

"Yeah, you are right. We should keep that in mind during the canvas. Maybe someone can tell us about him."

In urban neighborhoods like this, there are usually guys from the area who have made a business from a small yard job like Grace's.

I see a patrol car that has been guarding the scene overnight. I walk over to the patrol officer and say, "Hello sir."

" Hello detective," he replies.

"Do you work in this neighborhood?"

"I do, and I did not know the victim, but I would see her from time to time. She would usually sit on her porch and drink coffee in the mornings. There have been a few neighbors stopping by to ask if she was okay. Some were very upset that she was murdered."

Rob walked up and overheard some of our conversation. "Which neighbor was upset," he asked. "It was him, his name is Mr. Hill," pointing to a man sitting on his porch.

"Thanks sir," I say to the officer as we walk towards Mr. Hill's house.

"Hello sir, are you Mr. Hill?" " I am," he replied. "Do you mind if we speak with you for a few minutes?" Rob says.

"No, I don't mind, as long as you don't act like the other cops yesterday."

Mr. Hill, like everyone else in the neighborhood was an older man. Tall for his age and though he was sitting I could tell his back hadn't yet begun to lean forward. He sat straight, a tall man, and I guessed at one time an athlete.

"What do you mean? Did something happen yesterday?" "Yeah, cops came by yesterday, but they did not seem too concerned, assholes."

"I apologize, sir. However, we are back this morning to follow up on what happened across the street. Did you know your neighbor?"

"I have known Grace for fifteen years since I moved to this neighborhood. She was a sweet woman."

"When was the last time you spoke with her?"

"Two days ago, around this same time. She was outside drinking coffee, and we talked from across the street."

"Did she seem like there was something wrong?" "No, not at all. She sat outside until the guy finished her yard. When he left, she went inside."

"Did you know the guy cutting her yard."

"Nah, I've seen him around, you know looking for odd jobs, but I don't know his name.".

"Any idea where he may live?"

"No, I don't. I just started seeing him walk the neighborhood looking for work."

"What did he look like?" "6'1" maybe 180 lbs. soaking wet. Couldn't tell his age, but he looked like he'd just kicked a bad habit."

"Is there any more information about the guy or Ms. Grace you can tell us sir?"

"Grace was a sweet old woman, and she did not deserve to be murdered. I hope you catch the son-of-a-bitch that killed her."

"Thank you, Mr. Hill, and we will."

I had never been so unsure while talking to a witness. However, I tried to show a confident face.

As Rob and I walked through the rest of the neighborhood door-knocking, the crime scene images kept flashing in my head. Why would someone do this to an elderly person? She could not have put up much of a fight. But this was the modus operandi of my perp in the home invasions. Easy targets, I guess. Nevertheless, this was more than just a robbery; this was personal, very personal. Furthermore, we needed to find the person responsible before he or she struck again. My suspicions that this person was my perp from the other cases was growing with each hour. And despite my case going cold in the last two years, I now felt as if he'd come back and as they'd say in the movies, "with a vengeance."

It is now mid-day, and we are now a few blocks from Grace's home. Rob and I walk towards a house, and before we can knock, a middle-aged woman says, "just a minute officer." She then comes to the door, whispering, "I just put the kids down. What can I help you with?" I'm married, but I couldn't help but notice that she was probably the woman in the neighborhood who the men took notice of. Slender, autumn colored hair, a nice smile, though her children wrinkled the creases around her eyes subtly.

"Well, ma'am, I am Detective Chris Anderson. This is my partner Detective Rob Briscoe; we are looking into a case that happened a few blocks over and wondered if we could ask a few questions"" I said. ""Hello detectives, my name is Pam Whitten. Wait, does this have anything to do with the guy that was staying in the abandoned house behind us? H"'s been causing problems since we ran him off""

Interesting. "What guy? Do you know his name?" "No, but my husband called the cops on him last night. My husband caught him sneaking around our house. By the time the officers got there, he was gone."

Mrs. Whitten began to tell us she had noticed this strange man sleeping in an abandoned house two weeks ago. She explained how they had noticed small items missing from their home since he moved in. However, a few days ago, her husband's lawn equipment was stolen.

"What exactly was missing," I asked? "A weed eater, hedge clippers, and a lawnmower. Nevertheless, the mower is downstairs now. The officers found it in the abandoned house when they searched last night."

Rob and I both looked at each other, knowing we needed to search that house immediately. I tell Mrs. Whitten, "Wait here, ma'am, we are going to the house now. Where is it?" She points out the house, Rob calls for backup, and we hurriedly walk to the rear door. We enter the home through a damaged window and announce our presence. There weren't many vacant homes in the surrounding neighborhoods. But as the homes from the 1930s aged, fewer children and grandchildren of the owners wanted to upkeep homes that needed regular updating and renovation. This home though, one of the few remnants of the cottage-style from the 1950s, was in particularly bad decay. "Police, come out with your hands up!" With guns drawn, we began to search the house. The house's interior had been trashed, windows were smashed, and spray-painted murals covered almost every wall. The house smells of human feces, and only God knew what else. We began a room-by-room search but did not find anyone inside the residence.

What we did find was more valuable at this point of the investigation. In one of the bedrooms, we found prison release paperwork for Antonio Reed. Reed was a low-level criminal. His most recent arrest was for burglary and drug possession, for which he was sentenced to five years, for which he served only two.

He had only been out of prison for six months before discovering him. Rob and I cleared the house, and I took the information for Reed. After reinterviewing Mrs. Whitten, I found that Reed had access to the stolen lawn equipment when Grace was murdered. During the follow-up interview, Mrs. Whitten stated that she could identify him if she saw the person again. So, we went back to the office to research Reed's record, only to find his name was already in my robbery file. However, I had eliminated him early in my investigation due to proximity. But knowing he had been squatting in a house near the homicide, and my home invasions, he was now a prime person of interest.

I also learned that he was arrested days after Mildred's robbery occurred. That meant he was out during the time of all my string of home invasions. Moreover, it was also a potential explanation for why the home invasions suddenly stopped. I did not want to get too excited, and I needed to vet this information because we did not have any other leads on the murder case. Rob and I agreed we needed to find out if Reed had any connection to Grace. It was a long shot, but we had nothing to lose.

Now it was time to call in the big guns. The FBI does not usually work murders like Grace's, but when there is an element of a serial criminal, they are willing to aid. This case more than met their serial qualifications. I contacted my evidence technicians and instructed them to turn over all the blood samples taken from the home invasions and Grace's murder scene for comparison to Reed. My contact at the FBI assured me he could have the DNA comparisons back in a few weeks.

While we waited for the results, I created several photo-lineup spreads, and we went back to Mr. Hill's home. He looks at the picture lineup, points at Reed's picture, and says, "yeah, that is the guy I saw cutting Grace's grass. Did he kill her?"

"I do not know, sir, but we believe he has been committing crimes in this area. We need to keep this information quiet because he is not in custody." The neighbor nods his head in agreement, and I thank him for his cooperation.

I spent the next few days looking for Reed. He had not been seen since patrol officers searched the house, he had been squatting in. Mrs. Whitten had placed her neighbors on high alert, and they were calling the neighborhood cops if anything suspicious happened. There is nothing like retired nosey neighbors keeping the neighborhood safe! Over the four days, sixteen calls were made to the abandoned house. Most were kids from the area playing in the house, but the calls kept coming. After contacting Reed's parole officer, I learned that he was staying at a halfway house, and the parole officer could lay hands on him whenever I needed him. I told the Parole officer the case details, and he offered his full support in taking him into custody.

On the following day, I got a call from the FBI crime lab. The DNA in every case submitted came back to Antonio Reed. After that call was when I got a little excited! I did not have enough evidence to charge Reed with Grace's murder, but I did have enough to charge him with Mildred's home invasion if she could identify him.

I did not know if she could identify her attacker, but she could tell me Reed had never worked in her home or had reason to be in her home. After talking to her, she explained that she did not know Antonio Reed's name and was unsure if she could identify him from a photo. So, I contacted Reed's probation officer, and he immediately took Reed into custody and transferred him to me. During the five-hour interview, he was faced with so much evidence that he could not explain; Reed confessed to me how he committed the home invasions and the murder of Grace Garner.

Updating my Captain earned me a nomination for the detective the year award and a promotion to homicide as a detective.

Frank who owned the case before me only smiled when I saw him last. Perhaps he had a premonition. Perhaps, my initial instincts were correct in that I was pulled into the case thinking all along that I had indoctrinated myself into the investigation. Sure, I had been the one to ask my captain if I could review the murder case and cross it with my own investigation. But how did that murder come across my desk? Someone had told me about it. That was my connection and to this day I wonder how purposeful it all was. In my world there are no coincidences. It looked like there are at times, but the reality is that everything happens for a reason. Regardless of what brought me here. I was now a homicide detective, for good, for bad… This was a new path and something Anitra and I would have to work through.

The promotion to homicide brought on new challenges and new expectations. As a homicide detective you're considered the most elite detectives in the department. When a homicide detective steps on the scene, everyone expects you to know exactly what needs to be done. They all look to you for direction, even the supervisors. Being able to handle that type of responsibility is absolutely vital.

Not only must you possess a specific skill set to work the homicide cases, but you also must be able to see, understand, and operate around death and chaos daily. Those are the fundamental personality traits of a homicide detective. And they are key to becoming a successful one. I've seen detectives that possessed two traits, and I've seen some that possessed none. The one thing all those detectives had in common was, they never lasted long in the homicide unit. They would either ask for a transfer or they'd be removed from the unit after screwing up multiple cases.

When I was promoted to homicide, I made a pact with myself that I would never be one to give up on my cases. I also wanted to be the best we'd had in the position. Most of my mentors were former homicide detectives and most of them were damn good at it. I remember the stories they would tell me of what happens when you appear in the living room of a parent's home to tell them that their child is not coming home again. The investigator becomes the only person who can speak for that family. In some cases, your work and your voice fill the void left by the loss of your victim.

Knowing that only adds more stress to an already stressful investigation. With each update, every call, and every in person contact detectives should work to build a trust and a strong bond between you and your victims' family.

That's what happened in most of my cases. But I've had some families that almost blame me for the loss of their loved ones. Mainly because I was unable to bring charges against the suspects. I was never one to push the envelope of probable cause during my investigations. Meaning I wouldn't charge a person unless I was absolutely sure and could absolutely prove they were responsible for my victim's demise.

That was one of the standards I set as a detective. I've seen cases where the case pointed to one person, but the evidence pointed somewhere else. I've also seen cases where I knew exactly who was responsible for my victim's death, but couldn't prove it. In neither situation would I press charges, until I had direct evidence pointing towards a suspect, and subsequent corroborating evidence. That mind set sometimes frustrated my victims' families. But I always told them, I'd rather see one hundred guilty people go free than see one innocent person be convicted.

That mindset helped me develop, and keep lifelong friendships with my victims' families. Mainly Because I was able to solve the cases of most of their loved ones.

Chapter 2

At Home

After my first year in homicide, I learned there are some cases that will change your life forever. Those cases just stick with you throughout your career. When you solve them, your mind constantly questions why it happened. If you don't solve them, you spend the rest of your career, and some of your retirement wanting another crack at it. I've had a few of those, but there was one that I say truly made me a better man, father, and husband. My victim was a college student named Kayla.

Kayla was a beautiful, outgoing, intelligent, and ranked in the top three at the University of Alabama-Birmingham.

She volunteered daily for a senior citizens home, she took care of her grandparents, all while maintaining a 4.0 GPA. There is always that one case that will never leave you. And much like how an attractive young woman who goes missing is captured by the country on television, most homicide detectives have that one person they never forget. Kayla was the type of child every parent wishes to raise. She is the young woman we all know and love. You may have had a crush on a Kayla. You may have dated a Kayla. You may have even raised a Kayla. She was the one who entered the work force and was fast-tracked to an executive level. She was the special young woman who write and published a bestselling book before graduating college. She was the victim who was so perfect that literally every man with access to her was a suspect. I never got the opportunity to meet Kayla personally, but I'll always remember the night I first saw her.

That day was pretty normal. I was on-call, and stayed late at the office to finish some paperwork before going home. My phone rings, and I answer. "Hey." My face immediately shows a slight grin, it's my wife Anitra. She'd usually call after work before picking up the kids. Due to how hectic my days were as a detective; she would normally call to see what my plans were for dinner.

This was the routine but after the work day I'd had, hers was a welcomed call.

"Hey baby," I responded.

"How was your day?" she asked.

"Ehhhh, okay I guess."

I never liked talking about my days or my cases. Which is a problem with most cops; not talking about our days was our way of not bringing the other world we lived in home. I think back on it now and how draining it is for a homicide detective, hell, any detective to not talk about their work. Mental health isn't something we talk about on the force, but it should be. It's a draining existence and one we detectives try to keep contained into our own little world.

"Are you coming home for dinner?"

"I'm sure I will, what are you making?"

"It depends on if you're coming home.."

It's been a minute since I'd eaten a warm home cooked meal during the week so I decided I'd finish this stuff later.

"I'm headed home now."

"Good, we're having steaks," she says.

"Cool, I'll see you in about twenty minutes," I said.

As I hung up the phone, I couldn't help but think to myself, "well that was an easy exchange."

The days prior we had only seen each other in passing, due to the recent case that I was just closing. Plus, we were trying to work through and overcome a bout of infidelity on my part.

Nothing physical, but cheating none the less. After my first year in homicide my unit was chosen to be a part of a nationally known TV show. That show allowed me to become somewhat recognizable. That national attention opened the door for multiple women to reach out. While closing it on quite a few, I did converse with several women. Some by phone some through email, and some of those emails fell into the lap of my wife. That's never an easy conversation. For the first thing the younger me didn't recognize that I was cheating. Not initially at least. I sure questioned whether I should be talking to other women though. I also questioned if it was okay for me to go out for dinner with another woman. Even if it were casual. Or was it okay to talk on the phone with another woman. What were the boundaries of a marriage when it came to other women and, for her part, other men? They were not clear to me and as I became more visibly prominent, I didn't seem to question those boundaries. It felt wrong, talking to other women, but it also didn't stop me or prompt me to challenge those feelings. Anitra did not see me talking to other women in the same way I did.

You really don't know how much you loved someone until you lose them. After Anitra left, I quickly realized that she is the most important thing in my life. I was able to convince her to come back, but I'd not yet fully invested myself in the reconciliation. So, I submersed myself in work. I knew she had been pulling the entire load in my absence.

We'd been married then for eleven years, high school sweethearts with three kids (two were with us full time). But because of the time I was spending away from home our issues began to resurface. It was interesting that my career in law enforcement had been a rollercoaster of personal investment. When I first entered the force, I was gung-ho about it. I worked a lot of hours and was motivated every morning and stayed late into the night. Anitra was supportive of me. We were young, with small children, and needed that extra money.

I'd take on extra shifts when I could. I would work events and venues. And When security was needed for clubs or concerts it was common for event hosts to hire off-duty officers. Anitra and I were both invested in this way of life. But as the kids grew the life at home for Anitra became more challenging to manage, I'd given an effort to stay home more. I tried to avoid late hours and extra shifts. I wanted to be the provider and the perfect husband and father. But then we were short on money, and I started taking more shifts. Then came promotions. Then, I lost that path of being great at home and at work. Then I chose. Work.

Anitra suspected I wasn't as happy as I'd been early in my career. She still tried to do everything she could to make things better. Honestly, all I ever really wanted was her. Sometimes as men, husbands, and fathers we fail. Believe me, I know I've done my share of failing in my marriage. But tonight, was gonna be different, I'm going home to my wife, my son, and my daughter "Kayla." Yeah, you can probably see where this is going. Kayla.

So, I gather my things and start towards the elevator. But I remembered that I had a letter that was due and a phone call to make. This is usually where my screwups begin. I'd get busy and focused on what I was doing at that moment, and I'd lose track of time. Time during my years in homicide had become so precious. Because there was never enough of it. So, I decided, "ah it won't take long, I'll finish these up and then head home." I sit back at my desk and begin the process of typing my letters. When I look up at my watch again its two hours later and I'm still at the office.

I arrive home and both of our children run down stairs to love on daddy and show me grades for school work. While kneeling down to hug and kiss on them, I look up to see the look of disappointment in Anitra's eyes. "I'm sorry baby, I got held up."

She looks down at me with the *whatever Chris* look. She then tells the kids, "come on guys, get back in bed." She grabs my son's hand and walk them both back upstairs. Knowing what's about to happen, I head to the kitchen to eat my dinner. And to avoid an argument that's been brewing for days. See this was not the first time I'd stayed late at work when I promised I'd be home at a reasonable hour. It had become more frequent the weeks prior. Tonight, me being late – again - had only exacerbated the growing issue between us.

After piddling around downstairs for a few hours I decided to go up and get ready for bed. I put my gun and badge away and walk up the stairs. I know she should be asleep by now; I secretly think to myself. I notice the lights are off and the television is down, but still on. On my way up I stopped by the kids' rooms to peek in on them.

Hearing noise coming from my son's room I slowly ease the door open. "Chris Jr.?" He quickly plops down in his bed, but replies "yes sir?" Chris Jr. was the typical boy. A bit rambunctious. Happy, and easily excitable. He was also prone to test boundaries, though I have to say it was respectable about how he tested those boundaries. He knew the differences between right and wrong and was pretty good at managing how far he went.

"Aren't you supposed to be asleep son?"

"I am." he replies. I smile, walk in his room, and sit on the side of his toddler bunk bed.

"No, you're not," I say as we begin our rare laughing and horse play ritual. "How was school today bud?"

"Goooood," he says. Which is an indication that something happened, and he doesn't want to tell me about it.

"What happened buddy?" I ask

"Well, I kinda got in trouble today," as he holds his head down.

"Well, what happened?"

"I was drawing cartoons at lunch and the teacher saw me."

"Well, that doesn't sound too bad son, but what else happened?"

He then pulls out a three-page booklet of a comic strip with a long note attached.

"Well, son what did they say?"

"They want to have a conference with you or mom tomorrow." he said. The comic strip he'd drawn had army figures engaged in war with a super character he had created. Due to a recent school shooting they were cracking down on acts like this and I knew it. It may have been innocent to a kid in elementary school, but to adults and school officials it meant much more. The country as a whole had started to see a new spate of school shootings. Many considered this as a 21st century pandemic creating a dividing line in American politics. While it didn't start in Colorado, the Columbine Massacres in 1999 resulting in the deaths of fourteen students (including the two killers) and a teacher changed the trajectory of how the heinous nature of mass shootings moved forward in the country. Little has been done to manage school shootings and teachers, faculty, and other school officials were on regular alert trying to identify even the smallest of possibilities. My son creating a comic like this was something they'd focus on quickly. He was young, but rightly so, no one knew when the next Columbine would occur.

"Did you mean to hurt anyone buddy?"

"No sir" he replied.

"Did anyone else in your class see it besides your teacher?"

"No sir, I showed it to her."

"Okay buddy I'll talk to them tomorrow. Now get some rest bud"

"Yes sir," with the feeling of relief that he didn't really get into trouble. He hugs my neck then lays down in his bed.

I then walk over to my daughter, Kayla's, room, knock on the door "Hey baby are you asleep?"

"Not anymore, Dad."

I grin as I walk in and sit down in the chair in her room. "Well big girl, how was your day?"

"It was good, oh dad are you coming to my game tomorrow?" Kayla is my athlete, being five-foot ten-inches-tall at eleven years old we put a basketball in her hands early. Of course, in my mind I had images of her playing women's professional basketball. And why not? I mean you can teach skills to a child, and many will be athletic. What you can't teach, or train, or even provide is how tall your child will be. Height may not be the end-all to success, but a tall child, especially a young woman, will get the attention of college-level scouts, even at the tender age of eleven. In the world of scouts, an eleven-year-old 5'11" basketball player is less than two four-year classes away.

"Absolutely baby girl I'll be there. How are your grades looking?"

She replies, "come on dad, this is Kayla you're talking to." I love her confidence.

We both laugh and I shake my head at her. After our laugh I ask Kayla about the one subject she's uncomfortable talking to me about - boys. "So big girl, tell me about the little boys trying to talk to you."

Her head immediately falls into her hands, "Daddy," she says with the look of embarrassment on her face.

"What baby? I know it happens I just wanna make sure you're prepared big girl."

"No boys are trying to talk to me daddy," she said.

"Would you tell me if they were trying?"

"Of course, I wouldn't daddy," she laughs.

"All of the guys at my school know you, and are afraid, or they know me and are afraid, so I don't think I'll ever have a boyfriend at that school."

We both chuckled at her comments, and I said, "okay baby, I'll see you in the morning."

"Yes sir, goodnight daddy. Oh, and be careful, she's mad tonight," speaking about Anitra. I smile as I walk out, and close her door.

Now it's time to face the music as I head to my room. I secretly hope she's sleeping. We can avoid the brewing argument. I walk into the doorway, and guess who's staring at me? It's her, she's sitting up in bed arms folded in the *we need to talk* position. I walk straight to the closet and think to myself, *shit, here we go*. After removing my clothes and a quick shower, I jump into bed and turn my back towards her.

I can feel her piercing eyes on the back of my neck. Never saying a word, she plops down in bed and pulls the covers over her. Which pulls them off me. I don't budge because I know this will open the door to an argument, and I'm too tired for it tonight.

Chapter 3

The Call Out

After what seemed like just a few seconds I hear my phone buzz. I pick up the phone to check the time, it's 11:00 at night, and its already starting. I accept the call and say "Hello. Detective Anderson?" the woman's voice says.

"Yes, this is he," I reply.

"South Precinct needs your assistance sir. We have a signal 9." Of course, in my head, the call signal nine is immediately translated into homicide. I grab my note pad and begin to copy notes from the dispatcher. "Okay dispatch, I'm on the way" I tell her, as I sit on the edge of the bed.

I look over at my wife who's staring at me eyes wide open. "I've gotta go baby," I say to her. She rolls over, and pulls the covers back over her head. I throw on slacks, a shirt and tie, and head out. I wanted to stay home. I never want to leave, but I am compelled to. Homicides can occur anytime of the day or night and the faster we respond the faster we have a chance at closing the case. The problem was that eleven years into my career and we didn't have those money problems we had early on when I walked the streets or drove around in a squad car. I didn't need to put in the extra hours. But my career was different now. As a young officer I didn't have to work all those hours unless I needed the money. Now, as a homicide detective I didn't have an option. I couldn't pull a blanket over my head and cuddle up to my wife when the general rule of forty-eight hours existed to find a killer. I needed to use every minute of that early investigation to find the killer. I wish I could have explained that better to Anitra and my kids. Funny thing is that I think Anitra understood. And at the same time, she didn't.

By this time, as Anitra has buried herself in a defensive wall of blankets to hide her anger from me, I'm calling my partner and supervisors to notify them.

During the drive over I kept replaying my avoidance of the inevitable confrontation with Anitra. I kept trying to justify what I did. Talking about my day or arguing was not something I was good at. In my mind I was protecting my family by not talking about what I'd seen while at work. All my training taught me to leave work, at work. I didn't want to burden my family by talking about it, so I didn't. That was my coping mechanism. But no matter which way I tried to spin it, I kept coming back to me being wrong.

It was like when you have your good side and bad side arguing inside your head to justify your actions. But I must say in this scenario, even my bad side said, "you're an ass for that!" You know when your bad side says you're an ass it's time to listen and take action. I could only smirk and laugh as my sirens whaled while I drove up the freeway. I decided that I'd apologize as soon as I got home.

When I arrived on a scene, I always like to take a moment to take everything in before I begin to work. I see a newer looking BMW lodged on a concrete barrier still in drive. The car tires were still spinning. I notice a small group of young adults crying. Our uniformed officers were trying to console and interview them. The scene was a school parking lot, with houses to either side. Some of the residents had emerged from their sleep due to all of the police activity.

I then grab my customary stick of gum from my pocket, slide the gum into my mouth and place the wrapper in my pocket. Gum always helped me concentrate on the steps I needed to take with the investigation. I then walk over to the car to get a better look at the vehicle.

After walking to the car, I realize the tires were still engaged due to her knee pressing the gas. Her body was slumped down in the driver's seat, and you could hardly see her until you got directly over the car. The window from the driver's side was shattered. The remnants were scattered across the concrete.

I could tell that the vehicle had driven a short distance before it became lodged on top of the small barrier. Patrol officers did not want to contaminate the scene, so they didn't touch the car. Technicians arrive and secure the car from the possibility of moving. I then approached the car in order to start taking notes on what I see.

As I walk around the car, the patrol officers surrounded me and tell me their theories of how she got here. Listening to investigative theories was something I always tuned out.

In a murder case listening to theories only served two purposes, it makes the person giving the theories feel more knowledgeable about investigative work or it throws you off your investigation.

Either way I made sure to tune that kind of talking out on my cases. I pull the primary officer away and begin to talk to him.

"What do we have?"

"White female, 20 years old, when we pulled up the car was in gear. She was trying to escape her attackers."

"We got a name?" I ask.

"Kayla," he replies. I looked up at the officer, then looked over at the car. The impact of her name was immediate. That's how it works. I spent my entire career creating links and tying clues together that didn't look like they belonged together that a single name links me to a case. In this case, a young overachieving woman named Kayla hit home linked to my own young overachieving daughter named Kayla.

The young girl was still inside. I immediately began to feel for her parents. I could sympathize for them, more-so than I did for some of my other victims' parents. My daughter, her name is Kayla, and I had no clue as to how I would handle it if this was her. That's not a part of my world that I invite into my mind. A lot of detectives and cops will talk about how they see their spouses, children and family members in each case. That is how they can stay so dedicated to their cases. For me, I tried to not see my family. I didn't know how I would take it if I lost Anitra or any of my children. I don't know that I could continue to be a detective. I feel as if it would be a demotivator for me and take me down a dark path.

I walked away from the crowd of officers to gather myself and my thoughts. I knew from the onset that this case would take on a new challenge for me. After a few minutes I walked back over to the car and began to take notes of the crime scene. The area is pretty well lit, well-traveled, and has houses to either side. The parking lot where she was found was connected to a newer remodeled school, *maybe we will have some video* I think to myself. I write this info into my notes, and walk over to the officers still standing on the scene. My team members have begun to pulled up. So, I go over and begin to brief them on what I have so far.

We have a young female college student, nice vehicle, didn't appear she was involved in drugs, murdered in a semi well-lit area. After the briefing, I begin dispatching detectives to canvas the neighborhood surrounding the crime scene. I stayed on the scene to make sure I notated everything as it happened there. Early in my career I quickly learned that cases are won and lost on the crime scenes. There were no witnesses, no tangible leads, no video, nothing. This case was just like Grace's case, a "who done it." The reason why I think is self-explanatory. I had become so familiar with the term since my promotion that hearing it no longer phased me. It just meant I needed to work harder, and longer to close the case. In homicide investigations while on the scene you'll usually get a lead or two that needed to be followed up. By the end of the initial investigation in most cases you'll have a tangible lead in the case. When you don't have that tangible lead, you end up with a "who done it" because you have no idea who is responsible!

While on the scene I receive a call from our dispatchers. "Hello detective, this is dispatcher 9108. I have a possible witness on the line who states he was on the phone with the victim," she said.

"What's his name?"

"His name is David," she replies. Dispatch connected my cell to Davids's phone call.

"Hello David," I said.

"Yes sir, this is David," he replies.

"Where are you sir?"

"I'm in school about two hours away from Birmingham," he says. "Kayla and I were on the phone and the phone suddenly cut off."

I could hear how upset he was during the phone interview, so I asked, "would you mind coming to my office?"

"I'm a few hours away but I can be there by sunrise." Before hanging up he asked, "what happened to Kayla?"

Now that's not the type of news you'd want to give over the phone, so I say, "David I'd rather talk to you in person."

"Okay, detective, no problem I'll see you in a few hours."

When I start a new case my head repeats forty-eight, forty-eight. Obviously, cases can be solved beyond that time and every case is unique. But statistics don't lie. This idea of the first forty-eight was even perpetuated in a documentary-style TV show of the same name. So, as one witness or clue comes in after another, I feel a sudden burst of adrenaline swell through my body in hopes that each clue in itself can solve the murder. In this case, as the similarities to my own daughter were already impacting me, I wanted the case solved even faster.

Knowing this friend of my victim would be in town soon, I didn't want to waste any field-time I had. I continue to work the scene. After hanging up I think of how uniquely strange the call was. I begin to go over the possibility that David may be the suspect in this case. Who knows, maybe he actually shot Kayla, drove away then called police to begin to stage an alibi. In my head I play over the possible scenario. He calls her from the party and asks her to meet him in a secluded area. He gets upset and shoots her. Not very far-fetched and it has happened before.

As a homicide detective you never want to rule out a suspect. The facts and evidence of the case should do that. But I couldn't help but think about how strange that phone call was. If he is my suspect, he's got to be bold as hell to call me. And even bolder to agree to meet with me. Either way I need to make sure I get a very detailed statement from him and verify everything. This was the conversation I had in my head as I walked through the parking lot.

Now I'm a believer that there aren't any coincidences in homicide investigations, but this portion of the case made me rethink that. This young man stated that he was on the phone with Kayla when she was murdered so he had vital information about this investigation. I asked him to come in for an interview he told me he was two and a half hours away in school, but he was on his way. In cases like this who knows if he's a suspect, or just a witness. Either way he had information and I needed it.

While waiting for David, I decided to canvas the neighborhood with my partner and see if there were any witnesses. Door knocking at 1:00 am was hard but required. No one wants to be awakened by cops, because at that time of morning were only bringing bad news. But we had a case to solve, and I had to get the information as quickly as possible. after an hour or so, we had knocked on all of the doors in the neighborhood. Most didn't answer but leaving business contact cards on those doors could sometimes get the residents to call back. But for the few that did answer I talked to them at length about if they saw anything. Only one of the twenty plus houses we visited said they saw something. And this guy was willing to talk even at 2:00 in the morning. Truth be told, there is something about participating in a murder investigation that has people willing to talk regardless how early or late in the day it is. Witnesses, and many of them not witnesses in any regard, want to play a role. They want to call their buddies in the middle of the night, "Hey man, you have no idea how crazy tonight's been. Cops showed up to ask me about…" Maybe if I weren't a detective, I'd feel the same way. After all, we all want to feel like we're important.

"Come in detectives, my name is Ed Martin," the man said as he opened the door and stretched his arm out wide and inviting across his body.

"Mr. Martin, we don't want to take up too much of your time, but can you tell us what you saw tonight?" I didn't bother to wait for my partner and I to come inside or be invited to sit down.

Mr. Martin began with, "I just so happened to be up late after getting off work. Some nights I just can't sleep. I went into the living room to watch television.

While watching television I heard a pop and a loud crash. So, I get up and look outside the window and saw three people in a small car, light colored.

He stated he could not see their faces, but the car was a Toyota. He knew that because he had a car almost like the one he saw. The witness stated that he saw the wrecked car against the pole but didn't go over to see what happened. But he did call 911. I began to ask him several more questions, he paused to think and replied, "that's all I have detective." Before leaving the residence, I verified that he did make the 911 call and the dispatcher confirmed it. I left him a card and my cell number to call if he remembered anything else.

After leaving the residence I realized the young adults, college aged kids, were still on the scene. I walked over and began to speak with them about their involvement in the case. After just a few minutes of speaking I learned that they all attended the party with Kayla. None seemed very knowledgeable about what happened to Kayla, but they were all willing to be interviewed. I took all of their names down and asked, "how many other kids attended the party?" One young lady said, "about twenty-five of us."

I asked if they would all be willing to come to the Police Admin for an interview and they all agreed. Rob Briscoe, who's now my full-time partner is on the scene, he leaned over towards me and said, "Man you know we will need some reinforcements."

"Yeah, I know man, can you call them in?" That was our code for calling in anyone who was available to help, which was a common occurrence when working homicides.

Even when you were not on call you were still subject to being called. That was the job, we all knew it, and we all accepted it. I told the kids on the scene to meet me at the administration building with everyone that attended the party. The kids replied, "Yes sir" and they all went about the process of calling all of the kids in as they headed to their cars. We went about calling out the entire unit.

Chapter 4

The Notification

While waiting for David to arrive, and the party attendees to meet me, I had to do the most dreaded part of my job - family notification. It was never easy, and I always dreaded this part of the job. Mainly because I've been on the victim's side of the notification. As a rookie cop, I lost a close family member to murder, right here in my city. I was with my family when the detectives came to the family house and told us. The detectives seemed cold and uncaring.

I remember my mother, also a cop, trying to explain the detectives seemingly emotionless mind set to our family. She knew the two veteran homicide detectives from her years of being a veteran cop. I didn't know them, and honestly back then I really wasn't buying it. How could a person responsible for speaking for our loved one not care? The more the detectives spoke, the more I listened, the angrier I got. Until he said the one thing I couldn't fathom a detective saying, "well I think he was living a gay lifestyle and that may have been the reason for his murder."

This was news to my family, and we later found out he had his reasons for making that statement, but I didn't agree with his timing. My mother, grandmother, and aunt all sobbing together. I and my brothers consoling them, I say to the detectives, "sir, no matter what lifestyle he lived no one had the right to take his life." The detective quickly attempted to explain his comments but we'd all shutdown by then.

Eventually we forgave the detectives statements he made that night and luckily, we were able to get closure on the case. But I promised myself I'd always treat people with compassion. Especially during a time like death notifications. It's usually the first time meeting the detective and that's the one meeting that the family will always remember. So, it's imperative we detectives get it right.

It took me years, but I eventually learned a better understanding of why the detectives that night were so detached. Sometimes continuously submersing yourself in the underbelly of the worst crimes committed can affect your psyche.

Some homicide detectives must detach the human aspect of the crimes we investigate. That's the only way some detectives can consciously investigate the cases of this magnitude.

Homicide investigators are gatherers of facts. When making notifications you're still gathering facts. Also, as an investigator when you get so emotionally involved in cases you will miss something. Sometimes that something is so important that it could cost you your case during a trial. Most times when detectives are making those notification, they seem uncaring, when really their actively listening and investigating the case. After the night my family was notified, I always promised that when I went to homicide as a detective no family would ever feel the way I felt that night. My victim's families would know I cared, and they could trust I wouldn't stop until someone was brought to justice for their loss.

As my Rob and I drove to the location I couldn't help but think about how my mother felt when we were told our loved one was gone. I didn't want Kayla, my victims, family to remember me as a cold hearted, uncaring cop who just told me my daughter was dead. I rehearsed the conversation in my head the entire trip. No matter how many times I made notifications they were always hard. No amount of rehearsing or prompting can prepare you for it. Nevertheless, I still rehearsed what I needed to say, and be as compassionate as I could when I said it.

As we pulled up to the well-off home of Kayla, I made up in my mind that there is no easy way to do this. You've gotta just tell them. We park in the driveway, and exit the unmarked car. My partner looks over at me and said, "partner you ready?"

"Yeah man, of course I am," I say as confident as I could. You never wanna seem unsure as a veteran homicide cop, which I was. Luckily, he wasn't a part of the conversation that had already taken place in my head during the drive over.

As we approach the door, I notice all of the lights inside the home were on. This wasn't a good sign, it's now 4:00 am, we're about to give this family some of the worst news they'd ever received. And they were already awake? Somethings telling me we may be too late. Walking up to the door, I hear the whales of sadness coming from inside.

I knock on the door, and a man who I later learn is my victim's brother, Matthew, answers. He sees me, looks at my badge and gun and bursts into tears. I was immediately drawn back to our notification, and I felt that pain again. Matthew said, "is it true? Is my sister dead?" It was at that moment I hear another voice crying in the rear of the house. It's Kayla's father. I picture my son Christopher asking the police the same thing if they were to make this same call to our house. I picture me in the background crying and trying to hold back my tears and create any semblance of a clear thought. But it's not me having to do this. It is my victim, Kayla's dad. I put the thoughts at bay for the time being.

"I'm sorry sir but may we come in?" I asked.

With tears in his eyes, "my apologies sir, my family received a call earlier saying my sister was murdered. We've been calling her for hours, but we can't reach her." I'll touch on his comment with him later. But it does hit me. Was it someone from the police department who called? If so, I was unaware. But I also can't say it didn't happen. Miscommunication, especially early in a case happens all of the time. But I also wonder, was it a friend or someone who happened by the scene? Or did the family know about it because the family was involved or had insider information? It's never a thought I like to think about. Murdering or being a part of a family member's murder. But again, statistics matter and while each case is unique, most murders occur by someone that the victim knew and trusted.

"How are you related?" I asked trying to keep my demeanor comfortable and approachable rather than accusing.

"Kayla is my sister. I got a call from a friend of hers earlier tonight. He said he thought something happened to her, but he didn't know where. We have been calling for hours and driving the city. I made it to where it happened, but her body had been moved and the officers on the scene told us someone was on the way to the house. So, we drove home and waited for you. I hoped you would tell us something different, but I don't think you are. So, I told my dad a few minutes ago."

As he spoke, I noticed all of the pictures of Kayla's accomplishments displayed. Graduation, prom, family photos, and candid photos throughout the room. The pictures painted a picture of who Kayla really was. With every glance, my heart broke even more. I avoided contact with them when I could. My daughter was prominently displayed throughout our house. Anitra took great lengths to display our kids and their achievements. School pictures, awards, achievements, family pictures. They were all prominently displayed. Just then, as my eyes cutaways from a series of photos that looked like yearly school photos, Kayla's father then stumbled from the back room with the assistance of a woman.

With pain in his eyes and a mumbled voice he asked, "what happened to my baby?" After seeing her father, I couldn't help but think what if this was my child? This could have easily been her. My heart began to break as I sat down in my seat. My eyes were then drawn to a picture of him and her together proudly displayed on a coffee table in his living room. I was soon focused on one particular photograph. Because it reminded me of a picture, I took with my daughter Kayla as a child. Years earlier we'd taken a father daughter picture almost identical to the one displayed on his coffee table. I began thinking about the day we took the picture when I hear, "detective, detective."

"Yes sir, my apologies. Sir, there's no easy way to say this but we did find Kayla deceased tonight. As the words came from my mouth, he let out a scream of hurt and anger. I tried to console him but nothing I said could really ease his pain. After a few minutes he asked, "where did you find her" I replied "she was inside her vehicle, and we're still in the preliminary stages of the investigation. I want to make sure you understand, I work for you and your family. My only job is to make sure whoever is responsible pays for what they've done. I'll never lie or assume anything when we talk about Kayla's case. So, if you ask a question and I can't answer, I'll tell you I don't know. But I'll work my ass off until I find an answer. As it stands right now, I don't know exactly what happened to her, but I will find out."

"What can you tell us? How was she killed?" he asked.

"Right now, she's being taken to the coroner's office for an autopsy. By this afternoon I should be able to answer that." I replied.

The family asked a few other preliminary questions and we answered what we could. The father stood and reached out to shake my hand, I grabbed his hand, embraced him, "I'm sorry for your loss sir, you'll have my direct line if you need anything."

The father looked me in my eyes and nodded his approval, as he walked back to his room still assisted by the female. I could not help but feel the pain of this family.

After gathering information from Michael, I begin to question him about Kayla. "Do you know if she had a problem with anyone?"

"No sir, Kayla was the sweetest, easiest person in the world to get along with. I've never known her to dislike anyone. I'm sure if she had a problem with someone, she would have told me."

"Do you know of any of her friends that I could talk too?"

"Most of her friends were off in school now. She has a few friends at UAB, but none were very close," he said.

"Was she dating someone?" I asked.

"Not that I'm aware of. She and a guy named David dated but I think they stopped seeing each other a while back.

I do know they are still good friends. He actually was the person who called and told me something happened to Kayla. He called again called us before you guys got here."

"How well do you know David?" I asked.

"I know they went to high school together and they were good friends." Then he paused. A question came across his face as if he were putting his own puzzle together in his mind and eyes. I'd seen the expression hundreds of times in my career. "Wait, do you suspect he had something to do with this?" As quickly as his eyes introduced the idea, I could see them soften.

"Well as it stands right now, we don't know so I'm questioning everyone."

"I don't think David would do something like this to Kayla," he says. "But check with my mom, she knows him well." He turned around and shuffled through a desk drawer. He found a pen and Post-It pad then scribbled something down. "Here is her number, I've gotta check on my Dad."

"No problem, but I'm gonna need to talk to your father as soon as possible, I won't disturb him now." I assured them again that I would do everything in my power to make sure the person responsible was brought to justice.

"Thank you, detective," he said.

"No thank you for talking, we'll be in touch" I drop a few cards on the table and my partner and I leave headed back to the office.

As we drive away, I'm continually replaying the crime scene over in my head. "Something scared her, but what?" I say to Rob.

"You'll get it figured out, we're still at the beginning. But you know what we gotta do" he said.

"No?"

"Man, we gotta eat," It's now 5:30 in the morning and the sun is not up yet. We'd been on this case the entire night. I can't even begin to imagine how many tears Anitra had been crying into her pillow since I'd left. I wonder if she had even slept. She once told me that she often stayed awake at night when I wasn't home, fearing that I was lying dead in the street or being carted off to a hospital. Mid-thought, I'd forgotten that I've only drank a Coke through the night to keep me awake. Those fleeting and quick-transition thoughts were common. We pull over to the breakfast stop drive thru and head back to the office. There's something about a warm breakfast when you've been up all night. I don't know if cooks prepare food better or if it's the sleep deprivation, but breakfast always tastes better after a long night. The warmth of the food. The grease and inviting savory flavors of bacon. The biscuits were generous and soft. The eggs were fluffy, scrambled, with just a hint of salt and the delicate flavor of smooth butter. The sausage was juicy, and grits warmed my entire body. And it was exactly what I needed because this case was shaping up to be a twenty-four-hour ride. That basically means that I wouldn't be home for twenty-four hours. And these were the type of cases that I often wondered if being a detective was better equipped for someone without a family. The thought of my son's drawing from the previous day popped in my head. I needed to be at his school to talk to the teacher and principal. I sent myself a quick reminder that I hoped wouldn't be shuffled elsewhere as the case moved forward.

After scarfing down food, I don't know when it happened, but my body shuts down and I fall off to sleep at my desk.

Chapter 5

The Witness

I'm awakened by the lights in the office coming on. My sergeant, an old school gum shoe former homicide detective. He looks at me and says, "you look like shit. Where are my suspects?"

"I'm working on it sarge," I reply.

"Well, you won't find anything behind your fucking eyelids, trust me I've tried that. Go home and get some rest."

"I will, I have an important witness I need to interview before I leave"

"We got any leads?" he asked.

"Not yet, but it looks like an attempted carjacking or possible domestic. Just trying to narrow it down."

"Ten-four, I've already been asked for an update. I'll send that to the upper brass. Have you talked to robbery?"

"I sent an email earlier asking for all their recent robbery reports. They're sending them over today," I replied.

"Thank you, finish your interview and get some rest." He's a former homicide detective so he understands what happens during cases like this. But he also knows I'll run until I pass out. So, he keeps an eye on his detectives.

Five minutes later our secretary walks in. She's a mature woman and treats us all like sons and daughters. She looks over at me, "aww, was it a rough night? You look a little tired." "Well, that's an improvement. Sarge said I look like shit. So, I'm doing better already" We both chuckle as she makes coffee and I give her the low down on my case. In the midst of our conversation, my phone rings, and I answer.

"Hello?"

"Hello detective this is Nina the young lady from this morning who had the party. You asked me to gather the people who attended the party."

"Great, how many did you bring?" I asked.

"I've got everyone," she replied. Hearing that made me excited at the possibility that we may get a lead on the case, but my mind and body were exhausted after being up and out all night. Luckily, some of the homicide teams were rolling in and willing to help. I sent my partner down to bring them up while I set up a meeting with the supervisors and homicide team.

I usually conduct a meeting after a high-profile murder to update and plan for the following days. This way an investigator can get out and work the leads without pressure from superiors. I learned very fast after my promotion that if you keep them updated, they keep pressure away from you.

During the meeting I briefed the team on my case and what I'd learned so far. We had a deceased female student who'd just left a party. She received a call from a friend, pulled over at a well-lit school and she was murdered there. The reasons behind the murder we've not established. But we think it's either a domestic or attempted carjacking. As of right now I'm not ruling out either scenario. We have abut twenty of the party attendees in the office. They all need to be interviewed. I also need four investigators to go back out to re-canvas the scene.

I divide the teams up and we begin to interview the students. For hours we interviewed all of the students. One by one we separated and conducted the interviews making sure to verify and call out any discrepancies. And one by one they all pretty much gave the exact same account of the night. A group of party goers walked Kayla out of the apartment, saw her put the phone to her ear, and leave the location.

One of the kids told my partner he was headed back to his apartment after the party with several friends. While driving past the school they saw Kayla pulled over in the parking lot. Thinking something may be wrong they pulled up behind her to check and see if she was okay. They stated she gave them the thumbs up and pointed at her phone signaling that she was on the phone. The young man stated he had been drinking, and he wanted to get home, so they left her pulled over at the school. After receiving a phone call, they all came back to the scene, and saw the police. His statement was verified by several students that were in the car with him. All of the kids were interviewed by me and my team. After talking with them we determined that nothing unusual happened while at the party. Five minutes after walking the final party attendee out I received another phone call to my phone, which I answer.

Chapter 6

Talking to David

"Hello detective, its David, I'm downstairs" he said.

"Okay I'm on my way down."

Just a couple of hours after speaking to David, he was in my office. It made me wonder about his involvement in this case. Either he's not involved or he's a cunning son of a bitch, and this is his attempt to throw us off. Either way I'll be able to tell during the interview.

The young man was visibly shaken and upset. As an investigator you never want to automatically assume a person in his position is a witness or a suspect. Personally, I'd rather let his statements tell me which category he should be placed.

During my interview I could tell he and Kayla were very close.

He said "Kayla and I had been calling each other all day, but for some reason we kept missing each other's calls. Around 10:40 pm I called Kayla and she finally answered. I heard music in the background like she was at a party. I told her I'd call back, but she said she was leaving and asked me to hold on. I heard her as she walked to her car, and she got inside. She drove to a location and stopped, and I'm still on the phone with her. During our conversation she told me she parked at a school or something but just didn't want to go home yet. Our conversation was normal. We talked about how school was going and my girlfriend problems. I didn't like her being parked on the streets there, but I didn't say anything then." David began to uncontrollably cry during the interview, so I gave him a few minutes to gather himself before we proceeded.

"You okay David?" I asked.

"Yes sir, this is hard because I feel like this is my fault," he said.

"Why do you feel like that David"

"Because if I wasn't on the phone with her, she'd still be alive," he screamed, and began to cry even more.

In some cases, a guilty person would put on an act like that just to throw off detectives. It wasn't uncommon for the killer to be the most vocal and shed the most tears. For some this could be a practiced technique. For others, the guilt and love they had for that person was so strong that the guilty party couldn't control their emotions, but they could control their words. It all comes out as a very believable statement of loss. But David's statement has been very convincing. After giving David a few more minutes to gather himself I asked him to continue. I believed that he had nothing to do with the crime. But we didn't have many other leads available to us. So, I pressed him to go on looking or subtleties in his statement that I could probe further.

He said, "after talking for a few minutes more, Kayla suddenly stopped talking to me and began to talk to someone else. Her's and the unknown person's conversation was very short. When she gets back on the phone, I asked, who was that. She said, they think I'm here looking for drugs. I asked her who was it and she said just some guys. I asked her a few questions about the guys and exactly where she was. She said she was in a school parking lot near her college. I asked her to explain to me exactly where she was and that's what I told 911 when I called. I told Kayla that she needed to leave that area. But she cut me off saying, wait they're back. I then heard a loud pop and a rustling noise. I yelled for Kayla for several minutes, but she never answered." As tears again rolled down his eyes he said, "I hung up the phone and called 9-1-1, but I didn't have an address. I gave the lady on the phone the best description Kayla gave me, but I didn't know exactly where she was." David then called some of Kayla's friends who also attended the party with her.

One of them remembered seeing her parked at a school close to his house. That young man drove to the school, found her car, and called 911. He was one of the young men originally on the scene when I arrived and one of the party attendees we interviewed.

After speaking with David, I flat out asked him if he had anything to do with Kayla's death. Absolutely not detective, you can give me a polygraph, I will leave you my finger prints, and you can take my blood. I could never hurt Kayla; she was my best friend. I told David that I would set up a polygraph in a few hours "can you come back to take it?" Without hesitation he replied, "yes sir." Mind you I only asked that to get a reaction. And his reply was convincing. Although I was not ready to stop investigating David, I had no reason to hold him. I grabbed a card, gave him one, and sated "if you remember anything else call me." He shook his head, and walked out of the door.

After walking David out, I began to think about the media storm that was brewing about this case. I imagined the headlines reading like this "College Honors Student Murdered in Birmingham", "Beautiful College Student Murdered on School Campus." Alerts had gone out warning other students about safety. My Chief was receiving calls from the Mayor's office checking on the progress of the case. We were only hours into the case and the mayor was already checking in. That meant that the mayor's press people were lighting up his phone telling him that he needed to be in-the-know for this case. They expected the death of Kayla to grab nation-wide attention. I'm not saying the mayor didn't care about the death of his constituents. I'm sure it's the opposite and he cares a lot. But when the mayor contacts you within hours of a murder, you can sure bet that there is a reason. In this case, there was the death of an attractive and exceptional young woman who was murdered. That is what drives a media frenzy. That is what prompts someone, in the middle of the night, to let the mayor know that a young woman named Kayla was killed.

It was at that time I decided to start over, and go back to the scene. This time taking a few fresh eyes (other detectives) to see if we may have missed something. We arrive at the scene and begin to look around and see there are other buildings with video cameras. I also had our robbery detectives pull all of the car jacking's in the area. I send detectives to seize all surveillance video within a three-block radius of the crime scene. As they did that, I spoke with the school principal to see if the building has cameras.

During the meeting with the principal, he confirmed that there were no operating cameras at the school. But I was able to convince him to allow me to climb on top of the school so that I could check the roof. Who knows maybe the suspect threw a gun on the school to hide it? Since my promotion to homicide, I learned to do everything, even if it seemed unnecessary. With me, nothing was off the table when it came to solving my cases. Some may say climbing on a roof sounds like a stupid thing to do but my motto in homicide investigations is "what you didn't do will always come back to bite you."

My partner and I developed that motto because, no defense attorney will ever ask you during trial what you did to prove their client's guilt. But they damn sure will question you on what you didn't do. We've all seen or heard about cases on television or in the news where the evidence was right there. It just needs to be picked up or examined…but isn't. How many killers get away with murder just because of shotty police work. Sadly, there are a lot. Me and my partner were not going to let someone get off the hook because we missed something. I wasn't going to be that cop.

I've done everything from trash diving in a land field, working undercover to find witnesses, to working days strait. So, I've always tried to go above and beyond in my investigations. But this was taking it to a whole new level. Mainly because I'm afraid of heights. But duty calls, so my partner and I climb the roof of the school to take a look. After several dizzy spells, we unfortunately we don't find anything to help my case.

We are now sixteen hours into the investigation, and I don't have a single lead into finding a suspect, because none of the stores in the area had video. So far, I had a friend who was on the phone with Kayla. And we had people from a party that Kayla was attending who could give us some insight into what Kayla's movements were that night. It's not that we had nothing, but we didn't have much. And what we did have was mostly hearsay and guess work. Two things that hinder an investigation as much as they could provide help. I head back to my building with my partner to plan the next moves. After completely reviewing the case, we decide there's nothing more we can do. So, we decide to go home, get a shower, and some sleep. During my trip home I began to think about my conversation with David. David gave a very concise account of his whereabouts, including alibi's. Rob verified his alibi while I spoke with David. His statement also matched what we found on the scene. Kayla was found inside her vehicle phone on floor one fatal gunshot wound, nothing missing from the vehicle. Her last phone call was to David's number. No evidence a robbery took place. No drugs in the car. We hadn't identified a motive. I didn't know where the case was going, but I sure wanted to get there quick. I needed to close this one out and fast.

We were now seventeen hours in into the investigation, and I was nowhere closer to a suspect than I was when I received the call out. The fact that I didn't have a lead also bothered me. One thing I've learned the hard way was without a lead in the first 48 hours of an investigation, the likelihood of that case going unsolved doubles. And my window was closing very fast! I realized I needed to step outside the norm on this case. Press conferences was something I rarely utilized early in a case. Putting information out to early in an investigation can sometimes hurt the investigation. It also allows a suspect to see the information being circulated thru the media therefore allowing them to build alibi's or plot an exit. In this case I was running out of time and options. So, I contacted my sergeant and requested a press conference for the following morning.

Chapter 7

Headed Home

As I drove home, I couldn't get the case out of my mind. Flashes of Kayla's last moments kept appearing in my head. But the fact that I was finally about to get some rest actually made me feel good. I knew the argument with Anitra was still looming, Chris Jr. should be in after school care, and Kayla...............Kayla.... My eyes bucked when I mentioned her name. It was not until that moment I realized my daughter's game had already started. And I'd promised her I'd be there. I speed up the highway headed to her school. I began to think about how disappointing I was to my family by not being there. Especially Kayla, she's been the bright spot in all of this confusion. Plus, with this case it's made me even more sensitive to both my daughters, and our connection.

This has become a normal part of my life. Things go from zero to a hundred at the drop of a dime. Even-though I had adapted to operating in chaos, I didn't enjoy it. The one thing I hated was when I got so engorged in the case, I'd always lose track of everything else. It had also been a point of contention between Anitra and I for years.

As I pull into the parking lot, and walk in the gymnasium I see Anitra seated watching the final minutes of the game, with Chris Jr. a few bleachers over playing with some of his friends.

Anitra glances up at me as I sat down beside her. She leans over and says, "I called to remind you about the game."

"Yeah, I know, I've been interviewing all day today."

She smirks and shakes her head and says, "how was your day?"

"Aww you know people are always dying to see Chris" was my response and an attempt to make light of the situation. Anitra smirks and cuts her eyes at me.

"I talked to CJ's teachers about his comic book. He's been working on that for days now. He told the teachers that the hero was you. They were considering suspending him, but the principal squashed that," she said.

"Shit! My bad baby, I got so tied up at work today I forgot I told him I'd be there. Why didn't you call me?"

"I did."

I placed my head in my hands in frustration. I hated not keeping my word, especially to them. "It's fine, I didn't think you'd make it anyway, plus he's okay. After the meeting I ate lunch with him, and we talked about things. So, he's okay, mommy makes everything better" she said.

I chuckle and turn my attention to the game. Watching my daughter run up and down the court, I couldn't help but think about Kayla my victim, and her father. Whenever I had a fresh homicide, I felt bad for being home, able to enjoy your family, while your victims' families suffered in pain for the loss of their child. Good investigators cared about people, and cared about their victims' families. The great investigators knew how to balance their family and cases without either suffering. I was good, not great.

I hate to think of how I'd react if that were my Kayla. I wouldn't want my detective sitting in a gym, I'd want him out trying to find the son of a bitch responsible. Honestly, I'd want that person to pay with as much hurt as I was feeling. That type of thinking made me hurt for her family.

"Snap out of it Chris," I said to myself.

I knew I needed to focus on this small window of time I had with my family.

"How's she looking?" I say.

"Eleven points, eight rebounds so far, she looks good I think." Anitra replies.

"Wow I missed all of that."

"Yeah, you did" she replies.

I knew that was the doorway to our delayed argument, so I shook my head and wiped the sleep from my face. I knew it was coming. And no matter how I tried to delay it, this argument was inevitable.

Before I could reply, the end of game buzzer sounded. We all stood and applauded the girls as they shook hands and exited the court. As we stand Anitra says, "you look like you need some sleep."

"Well, I have been out partying all night," I sarcastically reply.

That's the asshole that sometimes slipped out after a long night. She shakes her head and says, "There are some leftovers in the fridge, why don't you go home and get some rest. We will be back home in a few."

"Yeah, I think I will."

A few moments later Kayla makes her way over to us. I extend my arms for a hug, and she gives me a high-five saying, "No, dad I'm sweaty and we don't do that."

"I see you did your thing tonight, huh?"

"I was okay, missed some easy shots but it was a decent night," she replied. Just then I feel something jump on my back. "Daddieeeeee" he says. It's my son Chris Jr.

"Was-sup buddy, how was school?"

"Aww Dad, I can't wait to tell you about what happened today," he says.

"CJ, daddy is going home to get some rest. You can tell him when we get there, Kayla gets changed up," Anitra says.

"Yes ma'am," they both say in unison.

Anitra looks up at me and says, "you only have about an hour or so to get a nap, I'll take them out for dinner."

She knew I needed rest. She always knew. Even though we were in a funk, and we really hadn't had a real conversation in days, she still knew. Guilt stifled me. I wanted to go with them and eat out as a family. It had been so long since we'd had even just a normal week as a family. But what is normal? I don't know that I'd ever had a week with the family where I was home at a reasonable time every day, or that I didn't have to leave in the middle of the night. I was exhausted and knew I needed to get home. So that's what I did. I drove home with sleep weighing heavy on my eyes.

After arriving home and grabbing a quick shower, I decided to pull out my case file and look over some notes while Anitra and the kids were away. As I looked through the notes, I realize that I had not spoken with Kayla my victim's mother. Michael had only mentioned her during our meeting, but he did say she and Kayla were very close. She was someone I really needed to talk too. As I looked deeper thru the file, I felt myself nodding off, so I laid my head on the table. Before I get my head down good, I hear my door opening.

"Dad? Dad? Where are you?" My son yells.

"I'm in here buddy," I reply.

He runs into my at-home office followed by Anitra and Kayla. He jumps in my lap and begins to rattle off everything that happened at school that day. My daughter Kayla says, "can't you even give dad five minutes before you start?" Now, I'm not seeing my daughter in the images I run through at work. I am seeing my victim Kayla as my daughter speaks. She's only eleven but she speaks as if she's ready for college. She is intelligent, and independent, and recognizes my need for rest despite how my time takes away from theirs. I am picturing my daughter as the victim.

He puts his arm on my shoulder, looks back at her, and says, "no!" Then keeps on talking to me.

I look at her with a slight grin and say, "aww he's alright baby." I kiss her on the cheek, grabbed him up and walked him up to his room. The conversation, although one sided, never stopped.

"Yeah buddy, yeah buddy," those were the only words I could get in. As he talked, I ran his bath water and listened even more. When the tub finished, he was still talking. I had to interrupt our in-depth but very one-sided conversation,

"Son, I apologize for not making it to our conference today. Something came up at work"

"That's okay, mom came," he replied.

"Yeah, but it's not good to make promises, and not keep them. As a man your word is your bond, and as a father I want to keep them to my children. I'm gonna try and do better, okay?"

"Okay dad."

"Okay buddy, go ahead and take a bath. And buddy, use some soap."

With the look of disappointment on his face he replied, "yes sir."

I walked back downstairs to see Anitra looking at the case file.

"What are you doing?" I ask.

"Is this what you're working on? This is the case that's been all over the news," she said.

"Yeah, this was the case I was called out on."

"Is her name Kayla?"

"Yeah," I replied.

"Oh my God, that poor mother. Do you have anything yet?"

"No sarge," I sarcastically reply.

The look in her eyes said it all. Within them I saw the frustration and anger of loneliness that had been contained for months. But now all those emotions had come to a head, and this was the opportunity to release it.

So, she did, "Look, I've not had a real conversation with you in weeks. And I've done everything plus some to make our marriage work. A weaker woman would have left your ass 1,000 times over. But I didn't, and I'm here! I'm working to keep us together! While your ass has avoided every opportunity to talk about anything. I'm 100-percent here and willing to work on us! But you've got me infinity shades of fucked up if you think I stayed in this marriage to be a single wife!" Her words cut like a knife, and I knew she was right. We talk about things like this with our partners all of the time. In fact, before Frank retired to leave me with my first murder investigation, he said the same thing. He was happiest about being able to have a normal life with his family. A "normal" life. Do any of us know what that means? Having a normal life after retirement meant that you missed your children's life growing up. Your kids were either out of the house or they were pretty close to graduating. I was wounded trying to even think of a way to accommodate Anitra. But she was right. She'd always been the astute student of the class on being a cop's wife. She'd excelled through the pain. She put the kids first and my career second while she let her personal needs dangle behind everything else.

And I realize this now because I'm older and much more mature. I only wish the older more mature me would have been there for this argument.

The older more mature me would've stopped, took a deep breath, and given an explanation that went something like this, "baby listen, this case has been extremely hard, and I know that you've been pulling the entire load in my absence. But this one is taking a toll on me. The hurt that this family is having to endure is unimaginable. I keep wondering to myself if this was my daughter what would I do? And I know that the past few weeks have been rough, but I can assure you once this case is done, I will do my best to make it up to you and our children."

Yeah, had I been the more mature me that's exactly what I would've said.

But I was not yet the more mature me. I had not learned the art of effective communication. So instead, I said, "What the hell do you mean? I'm working my ass off to keep us fed, comfortable and safe! There is no way I can do this job and not work the hours required! The long hours are a part of the job! We both knew that! There was once a time we were damn near begging for extra money. Now that we have some it's still a damn problem! What the hell do you want me to do?"

The yelling screaming and cursing at each other lasted for what I thought was an eternity. It was not until Anitra stopped mid-sentence and said, "Don't cry baby, mommy and daddy are just talking." As she walked passed me, I turned and saw my children crying as they witnessed our argument. She picked up CJ, grabbed Kayla by the hand and walked them back to their bedrooms.

Our kids had never witnessed us argue, mainly because we never did. But this time it was different, I was angry, and so was she. I decided that I needed to get away, so I grabbed my jacket and case file so I could drive and cool down.

After driving for twenty minutes, I found myself in the only place I could focus, my office. I figured I needed some time to calm down plus I could prepare for the upcoming press conference about my case. I placed my jacket and gun in my desk and sit down to read over my case file. After a few minutes of reading the sleep took over. So, I decided to rest my eyes for a quick minute.

I move to the office couch for a quick cat nap before I finished work. The office couch had become a safe place for detectives in my office. It's an old plaid colored, wooden framed, cloth piece of furniture that had been donated years before I was promoted. But I had become very familiar with the couch since I had spent several nights sleeping in my office. I learned that if I laid on my right side, I couldn't feel the broken springs in the seat. Yes, I would have preferred my warm bed, even with a mad wife beside me. But my body needed rest and it was going to get it.

Chapter 8

The Plea

After spending the night on the couch, I awakened to the noise of a working office. The media was chomping at the bits to get information on the case since they learned of the murder. My secretary sees me walk by her desk so she yells, "Chris, Chris can you come by my desk? You've got twenty messages from media trying to get updates on your case." I grab the pile of messages and lay them in my important stack of papers, I grab my office tooth brush and soap and head to the mens bathroom. I brushed my teeth and washed my face then walked to my sergeant's office to hammer out details of the press conference.

"Hey Sarge, I got no leads on this case. No DNA, no forensics, no witnesses. I'd taken a call from the coroner's office, and I found out that Kayla had been shot once in her head. Because of the wound, her death was instant. So, I told my sergeant, "the only thing I have thus far is a body and the fragments from the projectile. That's it! I need to do something to draw up more leads. This is why I wanna call a press conference."

Him knowing I'd been out for almost thirty hours strait working the case he replies, "well I was wondering when you'd get off your ass and finally do something. When do you wanna do it?"

I smirked, shook my head, and replied, "as soon as I can contact the family and set everything up."

Maybe we had a witness out there that we had not found yet. Hopefully, they would see the press conference and say something. When he agreed, I contacted Michael, Kayla's brother. After telling him my plan, I asked if someone could come down and represent the family.

"Michael, do you think your father would be willing to answer some media questions about your sister? It would help if someone who knew Kayla personally spoke on her behalf."

"Well, detective I don't think my father can do it, but my mother can. Actually, she's been calling for you to contact her," he said.

"I'll give her a call and set up the press conference for later today."

"Thank you, detective."

After the conversation with Michael, I contact their mother, Robin, Kayla's closest confidant. During the initial stages of the investigation, I did not know about much her. Michael wanted to tell their mother, which I understood. I asked if she could come in before the press conference and meet with me at my office. She was extremely shook up about Kayla's death, as you would expect. But she said she would push through the interview if it would help find who murdered her baby.

Now I know what you're saying, aren't all parents hurt by the loss of a child? My answer is yes. But I've dealt with some where the hurt is not genuine. Strange thing to say, but it is true. Many parents are at a loss. Emotion is drained from them. Some parents are just so tired of being a parent that while they mourn the loss of their child, they also find peace in moving forward with that responsibility. It's a harsh reality and it can sometimes blur a detective's perception. For example, if a parent becomes uncooperative or just wants to disappear, that maybe an indicator that the parent knows something more than they are letting on. If a parent doesn't seemed distressed enough then I might think they are hiding from something. This is only speculation of course, but it happens. And it happens a lot. Ms. Robin was different. She shed tears throughout the interview but there was strength within her eyes. I felt the love she had for Kayla during her interview. After the press conference was over, I asked her to come in for an interview.

It was there that I learned exactly who Kayla really was. She was a very bright and studious college student. She spent most of her time volunteering instead of partying. Ms. Robin Fanei stated each morning before school that Kayla would stop by her grandparents' home to check on them and handle chores like washing dishes and taking out the trash. Kayla was a very caring and loving young lady who loved athletics. That was the reason she attended the party that night.

Kayla's college soccer team was giving the party on the night she was murdered. The team members invited her to come on several occasions before. It was one of the few parties Kayla attended. It made me think about my own daughters. "How could these assholes do this to this beautiful young lady?" I thought to myself. What are the chances that this night, one of the few that she ever goes out, is the night that she is murdered? It all seemed so senseless.

I empathized so much I almost felt like she was my Kayla. As she spoke, my mind began to drift as I thought about what I was missing of my Kayla. All the missed games, dates, the nights I couldn't be there when she needed me. But I still had my daughter, and she didn't. I felt guilty because I still had my child, and chose not to be with them, but she would've given anything just for one more day with hers. In my head, I renewed my pact that this case won't go unsolved, and I needed to be a better father.

After getting some background I questioned her about Kayla, I wanted to find out more about her connection to David. He was still a person of interest on my list. I couldn't take him off my list yet. Though, deep within me I knew he had nothing to do with the murder. His alibi, his willingness to participate, and the fact that no one could imagine him doing anything to hurt Kayla. None of these things took him off my list, but at the same time, none of the other things kept him on my list. Ms. Robin stated, "Kayla and David were high school friends that spoke almost on a daily basis. I couldn't see David hurting Kayla ever." She provided some additional insight into their friendship, but it sounded like David was as much a part of Kayla's family as Kayla was.

"Was she seeing anyone?"

"No, not that I'm aware of and I'm pretty sure she would have told me." She replied.

"Any old flames she may have reconnected with?."

"Detective, I knew all of my daughter's boyfriends. I'm almost sure she wasn't seeing anyone, but I can't say 100-percent." It wasn't an answer that would satisfy my investigative appetite, but I could only accept it. Whether her mom thought she knew or didn't know wasn't a clear yes or no. I made a mental note as well as jotted it on my notebook paper to check in on potential boyfriends. Besides, for college-aged women, jilted boyfriends and ex-boyfriends were tops on my list of suspects.

Her statement basically confirmed what David told me during his interview. At the conclusion of my interview with her I was even more convinced of David's innocence. Her interview left me without any new leads to follow, and a lot more pressure to close this case. After the interview we both walked back to my desk before I walked her out. "Hey detective, you look exhausted" She says.

"I slept at the office last night. I'm leaving to grab some rest after I man the tip line for a while.

As I grab the stack of tips I was looking over, she scans my desk. Her eyes lock on the pictures of my family.

"Are those your children detective?"

"Yes ma'am, they are. This is my first-born baby, Kieara, she lives out of state, but we talk a lot. This is my son Chris Jr., and this is my daughter."

"Aww what's her name?"

I hesitate for a second, and reply, "her name is Kayla." I wanted more than anything to avoid telling her that. And her reaction was immediate as her eyes begin to swell, and she drops her head into her hands. I grab a tissue for her from my desk

. "I'm so sorry" I say to her.

"No detective don't be, your family is beautiful." She cracks a smile as she wipes a tear.

"Thank you." I didn't bother to go into the emotional toll I was putting on myself and my family. I didn't want to go into detail about how challenging this case was and how the similarities between her Kayla and my Kayla were almost too much for me to handle.

"Why are you spending so much time at work if you have a family as beautiful as yours at home?"

"I have a case to solve," I reply. I assume that everyone understands. If I don't solve these cases, then a murderer is out there. That person can and probably will kill someone else in the future. That next victim may even be one of my family members. That is often the motivation in what I do. It becomes a compulsion.

"Well, I'll say this, I'd do anything just to spend one more day with my child. This pain has been unimaginable. And I've truly learned that tomorrow is not promised. So, when you get home hold your family. If I just had one more day with my Kayla, I'd spend it just holding her, and telling her how much I love her. No parent should ever outlive their child."

Her words hit me hard. She reminded me of how absent I had been at home since the case began, and the fact that I left them after my blowup at Anitra. After she gathered herself, I gave her a hug and told her I won't stop until I find out who did this to Kayla.

We are now thirty-six hours into the investigation and my partner, and I are manning the phones for any leads to follow up. Three hours of taking phone calls, and nothing has come up. There is one thing I can say about the first forty-eight hours of an investigation. It's been my experience, if you don't get a viable lead within that pivotal first forty-eight hours, it is MUCH harder to close that case. We were almost forty hours since the call out, and we still don't have anything. This is the part that every investigator dreads, the waiting. After receiving no calls, we decide to go home, and start back fresh the following day.

A good hot shower and some rest always reenergized me when I was working a new case.

As I drive home, I began to think about my family. Anitra and I haven't spoken since the argument. We have not spent much time together since the case started. I decided to pick up the phone and call her.

After the first ring she picks up, "hey!"

"Hey baby, what are y'all doing?"

"Nothing. Chris Jr. and I just walked in," she says. This has been the normal conversation as of late, kinda dry but with some emotion. I've affectionately named it the, *I love you, but I don't like you right now*, mood. "Look I'm sorry about the other night, I had no reason to blow up like that. I was wrong" I said.

"You're right, you were wrong. But I could have been better also, so for that I'm sorry. I do feel like you have shut me out. I know there's something wrong, and you won't talk with me about it. That's not how we should resolve issues in our marriage. I can't operate like that."

I pulled my car over to focus on our conversation. "I'm not at my best when we're not good. This case has really affected me. For the past few days, I haven't been unable to get this case out of my head. The images in my head of my victim's body are sometimes replaced with our daughter and it's bothering me. At times I feel like I'm working my own child's murder."

The phone is silent for a brief moment "do you need to talk with someone?"

"We're talking now"

"No, I mean a professional Chris."

"No, I don't. I just need to figure this out."

"I'm here for you Chris, and your daughter is here also. In fact, she's at practice. Why don't you pick her up, and spend some time with her? CJ and I will be home when you two are done. Chris, are you ok? Because I'm worried about you."

"Yes baby, I'm fine. I'll grab Kayla and call you when we are headed home."

We hang up the phone and after a short drive I pull up to Kayla's gym practice. She excitedly runs to my car and says "Dad! Where's mom?"

"They are home, She asked me to pick you up. Do you want to go to the mall?"

"Ahhhh no, I'd like to take a shower first, and then we can go to the mall."

She and I talked and laughed the entire night. We went shopping and even caught a movie as a family. It was the first night in days that I could put the case completely out of mind and focus on spending time with my family.

I wake up the next day, check my phone and don't see any new calls about the case. I contact the unit secretary and I don't have any messages. The dreaded forty-eighth hour comes and passes with no new leads. For days I returned back to the scene trying to see if I may have missed something, but nothing was found.

Meanwhile more stories come out through the media; first local then national. This case even took me and my supervisor to the set of Nancy Grace. It was then that I begin to get calls from the psychics. Now let me give this disclaimer, I've never used a psychic on a murder case. As an investigator you're the gatherer of facts. Psychics don't offer facts. But on Kayla's case I had nothing and needed something, so I was willing to listen. Some of the psychic tips were outlandishly crazy. One called in and said she was murdered by spirits; others basically said the family was involved. We got so many that I asked for a detective that was specifically assigned to take the calls and make the reports for the psychic calls.

We knew we were still dealing with one of two scenarios in Kayla's murder. And those two scenarios had not changed since the beginning of the investigation, even though the jealous lover is seeming more far-fetched. However, as I have said investigators should never eliminate a lead, you let the evidence, and the investigation do that. But we still had no leads that would bring me any closer to a suspect. The days turned into weeks, and the weeks into months. And Robin called daily to check the progress of the case.

Chapter 9

The Lead

The phone calls from Robin became harder to answer. I never wanted her to lose faith or lose hope that the case would be solved. But secretly I was losing faith in my own ability to close it. Each time my phone rang, and I repeat "No ma'am nothing new," only deepened my loss of faith. The calls were hard for me because I was determined to solve this case.

Anitra and I had found some common ground, I began to communicate more with her about what I was feeling. I decided that therapy was a good option for me, and my therapist was a huge help. Even though I would never admit it. She helped me realize that I should communicate more with Anitra because the lack of communication was the biggest issue in our marriage. While we worked through those problems, Anitra became more understanding in my resolve to close Kayla's case.

After a month of investigation, the case goes cold, so I petitioned the Governor's office and the family for a reward. The total amount ended up being $50,000.00 I immediately scheduled a press conference with media to get the word out. I'm thinking, *wow! Okay, that should bring someone forward.* When news of the reward got out the leads started pouring in. That's when it comes in, I get a lead from someone who was an unlikely source but a dependable one.

A counselor at our County Juvenile Facility. The counselor states that he has been counseling these two young females who were homeless, and they have information about the case. It was the break I needed, so I asked if he could get the young ladies together to speak with me. We set up a time that day and he brought both girls to me at my office. I had hoped this was the break in the case I needed.

Now, the young ladies had a story of their own. That story was the reason they were in a position to be witnesses in this case. We will call them Latoya, and Latrice. Latoya was the 16-year-old older sister, and Latrice, the 15-year-old, very promiscuous younger sister. The counselor stated to me that both girls were in the state's care due to them being involved in several robberies in the city over the past year. Their mother had been incarcerated but had been released ten days earlier, and the girls were now back in her custody. While incarcerated the girls were living with a family friend who had custody of several male juveniles. All were suspected of being involved in criminal activity in the neighborhood.

The counselor stated that I may need to speak with the mother also, because she may have information on the murder. So, I call her into the office before I speak to the girls due to their ages. This is how things usually happen when you work homicide in urban areas. It's not all the glitz and glamor of your serial killer murder scenes. With serial murderers, you usually have science on your side or some sort of forensics. Urban murders, or robbery-style murders; detectives usually don't have much. It takes beating the streets and talking to people until you find something and then you must be ready to move quickly. That's exactly how it happened in this case.

When the mother arrives, I speak with her alone while the girls waited in separate rooms. I begin to question her about the case, and she really doesn't have much information about the case, but she fills me in on what the girls had been through while she was incarcerated. The mother, we will call her Mona, was sentenced to 190 days in jail for forged checks. While in custody the girls were placed with someone she considered a family friend. She said, while in jail Mona and the friend had a falling out. Mona says that the friend wanted the girls out of her home because they were disrespectful.

Mona later found out that the friend was allowing the girls to prostitute from the house to help finance them. She stated the girls told her that several of the other juveniles in the home were robbing people. Sometimes they allowed her older daughter Latoya, to go with them on the robberies. But they told them both about the ones she was not allowed to go on. Mona didn't know specifics about Kayla's murder, but she stated both her daughters did.

I then turn my focus to Latoya, the oldest. After gathering the preliminary information, I read her the super Miranda (or Juvenile Miranda) only because I don't know what she will say to me. She then begins to tell me a vivid story of how she and her sister were both in this home and that the so-called family friend was never at the home. But most of the criminally involved juveniles in the neighborhood lived, slept, and hung there at all times day and night.

Latoya says that she dated one of the young men. He was the leader, named Maurice. Her younger sister talked to another young man named Greg. He was with them also. She stated Alfred (another young man) was the son of the family friend and he was considered their cousin. Latoya went on to tell me about several robberies that she, Greg, Maurice, and Alfred were together when they occurred. Latoya stated that Greg was usually the driver because he was the only one that could really drive. Maurice and Alfred would approach the victims, and take the money.

I asked her what her involvement was, she said, "they made me stay in the car." Latoya said that she went on two of the robberies but one night they were all at the house and they were making plans to go out. "The night the murder happened they wouldn't let me go," she said. "They left the house around 9:00 pm. It was Maurice, Alfred, and Greg. They returned around 1:00 the next morning." She remembered because she was up watching late night television. I asked her if she remembered the program, which was something I did just to verify the statement. She told me what it was, and my partners verified it.

Latoya said she saw them all outside talking when they returned, and she joined them. When she walked out, they all got quiet for a few minutes. But after a while they began to tell her about that night. Latoya says the first one to mention anything was Alfred, and he was egging Maurice on. Maurice said, "man I had to dome that Bitch." The fact that she said "domed" sent up a flag. On the streets (domed) means to be shot in the head. Kayla had been shot in the head, and that information was not public information.

At that time, she didn't know exactly what Maurice was talking about, but within the following days with all the news coverage she found out. The following morning Latoya and Alfred were watching the news and that's when he confessed to her. Latoya said Alfred told her all three were together and they were looking for a car to take. They saw a nice-looking small car and a female was inside it. When they saw the car park, he told Greg to go take it. Greg got scared and came back to their car and pulled off.

Alfred said they then pulled around the school and saw she was still there, so Maurice went to the car. Alfred said the girl then pulled off and tried to run over Maurice, so he shot her. Alfred said, "that's the girl they talking about on the news."

Latoya said she didn't really believe him until the following days they all started acting really strange. She said she saw Maurice with a newspaper article of Kayla, and he put it in a shoe box. When he placed the article in the box, he told her, "this is my first kill."

At this point I'm livid! "Why didn't you call police? You just sat there and listened at them admit to killing this young girl and didn't say anything." It was moments like this that I had to put things into perspective. I couldn't always do it though. She was young, naïve, scared and who knows what else. But this case had been going on for months and an innocent person died. How many other people would die due to these guys? Latoya probably didn't think that far. She probably thought this was all a one-off situation. If she kept her mouth closed, she wouldn't be bothered by what happened and in time the case would go cold, and she could move on with her life. It's frustrating but a part of the job.

She responded, "Detective, I was scared. They could have killed me, and no one wouldn't have known nothing. My mom was gone, this was all we had." she replied.

It was then I realized that she was right. These girls were still children and living in a situation and conditions that most adults know nothing about. I also realized, these two would be the only real way there would be any chance of prosecuting the assailants.

I calm myself down and grab Latoya some tissue to wipe her tears so we can finish the interview. "Why now, after all these months would you come forward?" I asked.

"I wanted to do what was right," she said.

Now my thoughts were, "you should have wanted to do what was right months ago," but I had to remind myself they were children. Also, if there was any hope of solving this case you would need their testimony to bring any charges. I bring myself back into detective mode. I ask her, "would you be able to identify these guys?"

She replies, "yes." I have my partner make up some photo lineups and she identifies all three without hesitation.

This is it! Her statement was a huge break in the case! I went from having absolutely nothing to having a lot more leads to work on. But I still needed to talk to her sister. I then begin with the younger sister Latrice. Latrice stated she wasn't there when they returned after the robbery attempt. Although she overheard Maurice talking about the murder. She heard him saying he wanted the car, but he shot her because she tried to run him over. Latrice said, "he wouldn't answer my questions, but he kept admitting he shot her."

Within the following days they kept talking about it and kept the news articles and the gun. She said they were in a shoe box inside the house. "The gun is inside the house, in the shoe box" I asked. "Yes, that is where Maurice kept it" she replied. Some may say, "that's all you need! Now get some arrest warrants and GO GET'EM!!" Wait…stop… What do you really have detectives? You have two juvenile criminal prostitutes that are accusing these fine young men of MURDER, without any real evidence. That's what any rookie defense attorney would argue. And honestly, they would be right.

We have no solid evidence in the case. The statement from Latoya saying she heard Maurice say, "I domed that bitch." Knowing that information was kept from the public, and both girls having specific details about the murder helps. But I wouldn't rest my case on it. Latoya knew of specific robberies that the suspects had committed so I obtained warrants for their arrests in those robberies. I gathered as much information from the girls as they could give, and I obtained a search warrant for the house. The search would be for the only physical evidence that so far existed in this case. Finding the shoe box of articles, and the murder weapon would help authenticate the girls' statements if it existed. Taking these suspects into custody would not be a simple task.

Now it's time to call in the big guns. In my city we have a group of Tactically Trained Investigators that only hunt down our most violent criminals. The Criminal Response Team or C.R.T. At the time, they worked directly with the US Marshals office. Throughout the investigation they were assisting me. As matter of fact all the alphabet crews were assisting (FBI) Federal Bureau of Investigations, (ATF)

Alcohol Tobacco and Firearms, (ABI) Alabama Bureau of Investigations, and the US Marshals, but when the case went cold, they all had to pull off. Now that we have new leads and suspects they were all ready to move. I gave the Marshals the names and information and asked them to set up twenty-four-hour surveillance on the suspects and the houses until we were ready to move. The FBI sent in a tactical team and set up a Science and Technology center in their office for any evidence we needed processed quickly. The ATF made agents available to us if we needed gun information that we found during the search. This was all setup in a matter of hours after the girl's interview.

With all this activity around the office I get a call from my supervisor, who's been monitoring the case's progress carefully. My supervisor wanted a briefing about the entire operation before we made a move. While frustrating, it's understandable. Because if something went wrong it would be them explaining and not me. So, I gave everyone assisting me a break while my partner and I briefed the brass about the operational plan.

After the briefing, I walk out and realize that the only way I can get charges is if I get either an admission or a confession from all of them. Which is a task within itself, but I refuse to let this opportunity slip away. The plan was to wait until day break and hit the houses simultaneously at first light. There were three target locations. Alfred and Maurice were confirmed at one location, but Greg was believed to be at one of two locations. It's about 5:00 pm now, so my partner and I decide to go home, our meeting time was 4:00 am. I couldn't believe it. And actual time with my family. In fact, when I got home early Anitra looked at me as if I were an intruder. "Did you forget something?" She'd asked.

"No. I'm home tonight."

"Uh, huh," The expression on her face told em everything I need to know. She didn't believe it.

"I'm serious. Nothing is going to take me out of this house tonight." I smiled and she reciprocated. Though I could still see the doubt in her eyes.

"Kids," Anitra calls, "Let's eat."

My phone rings. It's the P.D. Anitra drops her shoulders. *I didn't think you'd stay*, was written all over her. I answered and CRT detective got me up to speed.

My kids walked into the kitchen, surprised to see me at the table. I waved at them. Anitra was putting food on the table as she stared at me. I'm sure she was half expecting me to stand up and take off. But I wasn't leaving. I figured even with this call, taking a few hours with my family would no longer hurt the case.

The detective told me they saw Greg in a stolen car and began to chase him. After a short chase and wreck, he's apprehended without injury, and he has a gun inside the car. I say to the arresting officer to "take him into custody and transport him to the jail on his outstanding charges. I'll question him in the morning" we hang up the phone and I sit down for dinner.

Anitra looks over at me, "Really?" she asked.

"Really." I responded.

She could not believe I was actually staying home for dinner, and spending time with them as a family. Over the past months of the investigation, I was more open about what was happening with the case. During dinner I told her about the break I received, and Greg was now in custody. After the meal, I helped in the kitchen. Chris Jr. was in and out talking and playing, while Kayla stayed at the table finishing homework and conversing with me. After a few minutes I noticed a worried look on Anitra's face.

I walk over embrace her by the waste, and say "what's wrong." "Look I love having you here right now. The smiles on our kids' faces are priceless. I don't see them this happy until you're here. But I cannot help but think about Kayla's mother. She will never see her baby again. I don't know how everything works with your cases, but I do know the kid they have in custody is important. So, if you need to go, then go. We will be here waiting for you until you get home."

She was right, interviewing Greg was extremely important to the case and it needed to be done as soon as possible. I looked her in the eyes, kissed her on the cheek, and said I should probably go. Anitra then looks at the kids and say guys come say bye to Daddy he needs to go back to work, he'll be back soon. Chris jr. runs into the kitchen hugs my leg and says, "Ok bye dad!" Then runs back out; Kayla, grabs her things, kisses me on the cheek and says, "bye daddy, I'll see you when you get back." She then walks up into her bedroom. Anitra now facing me with a slight grin says, "ok baby, I'll see you when you get home, and be careful." She then gives me a loving kiss on the lips. I smile back at her walk into my office grab my gear, and head to my unmarked car. Knowing things were good at home and they were all safe gave me a since of calm and confidence. And confidence was what I needed going into this interrogation.

When I got to the police station, I began to question Greg about the cases I had against them. Out of the three suspects, Greg was the least criminally inclined, but he lied the entire time I spoke with him. I was able to get Greg to confess to four robberies. But we went back and forth for a few hours about the murder. He lied until I let him know that I would have them all in custody in the next few hours. I told him, his partners would talk, they would place all the blame on him, and he'd be left on his own.

I left out of the room leaving him alone for a brief time period, until I heard the knock at the interview room door. Greg wants to talk now. He gives me a full confession stating that he, Maurice, and Alfred had been out that night looking for a car to get. They see Kayla and follow her. She was alone and had a nice car and they wanted it. Greg says they were prepared to follow her for a while, but she pulled over in the school parking lot. That's when they saw the opportunity. Greg says he was driving but Maurice wanted him to rob her. He said he didn't want to, but he reluctantly approached the car and asked the girl if she wanted to buy some weed. Greg said she shook her head like, "no" and he walked back to the car and pulled off.

Maurice was mad at him and told him to go back, so he did. Greg said the car was still there. So, he pulled behind her again and Maurice pulled the gun and just shot her, but she pulled off and wrecked. Greg says Maurice jumped back in the car and he pulled off. Greg said he thought she was still alive until they watched the news the next day and saw she was dead. I asked Greg what he did after they left the location, and he said he dropped Alfred and Maurice off at Alfred's house and left. He could not remember if he stayed at Alfred's house for a few but said he may have. That was it. I needed him to implicate himself and he did it.

By that time, it was almost 3:00 am and we had a 4:00 am call in, so I had Greg transferred to jail and I grabbed a little sleep at my desk. 4:00 am came and I was ready to roll. We conducted a 5:00 am briefing, gave everyone assignments and we went to the location. Minutes before arriving at the residence I get a radio call from the Marshals who were still conducting surveillance. The transmission stating, "target has left the location, should we take him down?" I give the order to take him down while we continued on and hit the house.

After a few minutes I hear radio traffic stating targets in custody plus six others detained. The house was full of teenagers just like my witnesses said it would be. The girls also told me about the squalor that the house was in. But when I arrived, I found out, six teenagers were all sitting outside the house with officers guarding them. One of them, a teenage female, is cursing officers loudly. The others begin to get loud also, but when my partners and I walk to the porch most of them began to calm down. Everyone except one female; she got even louder! I go over and try to calm her down, but she's not having it. The young lady begins to curse me and anyone that will listen. I tell officers to place her inside a vehicle and transport her to the building. As I approach the other teenagers, I recognize some of them from my days in robbery. I knew we were on the right track then.

What I've found is most teenage criminals in my city run together so if you have one robber in a group usually a few of the others have committed a robbery with that person or knows about some of the crimes that person has committed.

With these kids I still needed information, and I didn't know what they knew. So, the ones I could charge I took them into custody. The rest, if their parents came to the scene, we released them at police headquarters after being interviewed.

My partners and I then entered the residence and the squalor these kids were living in was atrocious. Clothing, old food, and insects were everywhere. The smell was something awful. The house was even worse than I could imagine during the interview with the girls. But I knew we were there for a reason. There was evidence inside that house, and we needed to find it. So, my partner and I ditched the shirts and ties, threw on the trusted zip up jackets with gloves and started the search.

We sifted through the garbage, old clothes, even something that looked and smelled like human feces. Each room was more of the same thing. The heat was so bad inside, that we had to take breaks just to gather ourselves. While I was out conducting the search warrant, I had a group of detectives talking to the occupants of the house; everyone except the suspects. Here is the part where I tell you about police procedures and best practices in a homicide case.

As I have said before, A good homicide detective is a collector of facts, a gatherer of evidence. Armed with facts and evidence he can implement a strategy to obtain a confession or admission to the crime he or she is investigating. Sometimes gathering that evidence takes time, A LOT of time! So, when I see cases where defense attorneys say, "Cops kept my client for several hours." I just look and give my side grin and shake my head.

Because honestly those same defense attorneys attempt to make cops look foolish when evidence is missed. So, I always made it a priority to take as much time as possible for information gathering. I do a disservice to my victims and their families when I rush my investigation. So, I never rushed.

Some of the kids had been at the building for hours so I arranged for food for the ones that were still there. The rest were released to parents and guardians, while I finished the search of the house. My team and I went through every inch of that house but didn't find the newspaper article that the girls mentioned. We found several guns that no one ever knew who they belonged to (none were the murder weapon). I decided to keep the house locked down until I could get more info from my team and the suspects. So, I posted uniformed officers at the residences to continue the search. In investigations this large, I needed to hold on to everything I had. I left the location to speak with the suspects we had in custody.

The first suspect I decided to speak with was Alfred. He was more of a follower, and he didn't appear to have much of a criminal history. So, experience tells me he should be the first person I talk to. Maybe he'll be willing to give me some information.

Chapter 10

Alfred

Alfred's lack of a criminal history bothered me. Kids his age don't usually go straight to murder. So, either he was a criminal anomaly, or he's been involved in some crime and had not been arrested. Either way that's where I'm starting. Plus, according to my witnesses he seemed to be the least culpable in this murder. I sit down with him, and we begin our conversation.

After just short of an hour of general conversation I hit him with the information Greg told me about the murder. "Alfred, listen I've been doing this a long time and I'm a fair man. I'm fair when I'm being told the truth. So, I'm gonna ask you some questions about Maurice, Greg, and you. I want you to be truthful. Even if what you tell me is bad, I want the truth"

"Detective I didn't do this. I wasn't with him. I don't know what Greg is talking about," he responds.

"But I have witnesses that say that there were three people in that vehicle," I tell him.

"Look, if you were there and you didn't have anything to do with this murder tell me that. But don't tell me that you weren't there. Because I'm about to talk with Maurice. And I'm sure Maurice is going to say something different."

He looks down, places his hands in his head, "yeah detective I was there but I didn't know they were going to shoot her. It was Greg who shot her," he said. Alfred then begins to tell me his version of how the murder actually happened.

"That night we were just out looking for some easy money. We were all broke and hungry, so we went out looking for a lick."

Now if you don't understand what the term "lick" means, in street terms, it is a robbery. After hearing that, I knew I had something I could hang my hat on. But I needed more from him so, I let him talk. "We saw the BMW, and the girl, and we knew we could get some money for the car," he said. "We follow until we see her pull over at a school. So, we pull into a parking lot across the street and stop. Maurice tells Greg, go get it. Greg tells him, nah man you do it I'm driving. They argue back and forth for a few minutes until Greg said okay, man, damn. Greg puts the car in drive and pulls up behind the girl, and gets out. He walks over to the car, talks to the girl, and then comes back to the car. "I saw Greg get out of the car and walk over to the BMW. And a few seconds later he walks back, gets in the car and we drive off" he said. "He and Maurice start to argue about what happened."

The whole time I'm just listening letting him talk, trying my best to hold back the anger I feel. In my head my mind is flashing back and forth between the pictures of my Kayla and my victim Kayla. This could have been my child; I'm thinking to myself, Kayla my victim was someone's child, sister, and granddaughter. You stood by and let this happen! Why didn't you say anything to stop this? The anger of all the sleepless nights, door to door knocking, and holding this mother as she wept for her daughter. Not to mention everything I was missing at my own home!

All these thoughts were swirling through my head when I hear him say, "so, I dozed off to sleep."

"What?" I said.

"You went to sleep, while they are arguing in a car?"

"Yeah, I was tired," he said.

"That's bullshit! And you know it! Why start lying now?"

"There's no way you go to sleep minutes before a robbery. Who are you protecting? Because God knows they won't protect your ass."

Just then I remember the witnesses said Maurice and Alfred are close, they're cousins, but act like brothers.

"So, you're gonna protect Maurice?"

"I get it now; Maurice is your family. By saying you went to sleep, you wouldn't be a witness against him, right?"

"Nah man. I ain't trying to protect nobody."

"I was sleep the whole time."

After looking down, I say "Look son, you're about to ruin your entire life. Did you ever try and talk them out of it?"

"Nah, that was on them. If they did something, but I didn't have nothing to do with it."

Things got so heated in the room and I needed to gather my composure.

"We need to take a break; do you need something to drink or eat?"

"Do y'all have a soda?"

"Yeah, I'll get you one, want some chips also?"

"Yes sir," he replies.

I grab the chips and soda and take it back to him. While he eats, I sit in the conference surveillance room and watch the screens with suspects and potential witnesses in them. When rooms get heated like that its always best for me to pull away and take a break.

I downed a few gulps of soda as the FBI guys and my partners talk to the other witnesses in the interview rooms. Interview after interview I hear everyone deny any involvement in the murder, but all had some second-hand knowledge about it. Nothing that would solidify my case, but most of the pieces fit. So, I decided to move on to the final suspect in the case. According to my witnesses he's the most culpable of the three, and I thought he'd be the hardest to crack.

According to the girls, he was the leader of them all. He called the shots, everyone else just followed. So going in, I know I need to get him talking and talking a lot.

I go to his door, knock twice, and walk in.

Maurice

"Hello Maurice, I'm Detective Anderson. I need to talk to you about a case I'm working," I say.

"What case?" he asks.

"Well, we will talk about that."

"Okay," he replies.

I begin with asking him general questions about his personal life. I learned that he'd been staying with friends for the past few years. He'd stopped going to school around the seventh grade and left his mom's home shortly thereafter. He told me that his mom was strung out on drugs, and he had not seen her in months. He was one of six children, and only three of his siblings were still alive.

"What happened to your other siblings?" I asked.

"They're dead," he replied. I could see the emotion in his eyes, so I shifted to his living relatives.

"Where are the others?"

"We were staying with my Grandma, but I left there a long time ago."

"Well, how are you taking care of yourself?"

"I can take care of myself. I'm a grown man."

"Maurice, you're eighteen years old, that's hardly grown."

"Man, you don't know me! Where is my cousin? Man, I'm ready to get outta here. So, what do you wanna talk about? What case?"

"Hold on man," I cut him off, "have I raised my voice? No, I've not, I've only been respectful to you, and I expect the same respect. Is that understood?"

He looks back at me cuts his eyes and replies, "yes sir."

That one reply gives me a little insight to what type of personality he has. In the thirty minutes we'd been talking Maurice had given me enough about him to know certain things about his upbringing and personality. He was protective over the people he cared about and hated being talked down to.

Even though this kid may be a killer he has some respect. As long as we can maintain the respect, I'll adjust the way I conduct the interview.

Now that I have a plan, I needed to get him talking about Kayla's murder. We small talk for a few more minutes and then I hit him with the facts of the case.

As an investigator you never wanna reveal what you know too quickly. The object is to get the suspect talking. While he talks, you listen and call bullshit when you hear it. So, without revealing names, I let him know some of what I know.

"Maurice, I'm gonna cut to the chase. Your name has come up in a case I'm working. Everyone involved is pointing fingers, and most of those fingers lead back to you. Now if you tell me that you're not involved and I have proof otherwise, then I have no choice but to believe what they are saying. And I don't want to do that if they are just saying it to save their own asses, and throwing yours under the bus. So, I'm only giving you one chance to tell me the truth. Tell me what you did?"

"Wait, detective, they're saying I did everything, even my cousin?" he asked.

"Well let me say this Maurice, I'm not going to tell you who said what because if you're telling the truth and they are telling the truth, your story's will match. But I will say this, everyone says you were with them. So, you tell me, who should I believe?" I ask.

"Believe me detective, because I didn't have nothing to do with this," he replied.

"Well wait, who's idea, was it? Was it Greg's, Alfred's, or yours?"

"See it wasn't like that. We were just out riding so it wasn't like somebody's idea. We were just out."

"Okay, who was driving?"

"It was Greg's car, so he was driving."

"What kind of car were y'all in?"

"Greg had a little Toyota or a Nissan. I can't remember exactly but it was one of those."

"Okay, go ahead"

"Greg said, man look at that car right there. So, Greg started following her through south side. Then she parked and we parked across the street watching her. Greg said I'm finna get that. So, he pulled up to the girl like he was trying to talk to her or something. A few seconds later he came back and got in the car and drove off. He told Alfred that she was on the phone, so he wasn't gonna do it. Alfred started calling him scared. I got sleepy so I dozed off and went to sleep. I didn't wake up until we got back to Alfreds house."

"Wait a minute. You missed a whole lot" I said. "Where were you sitting?"

"I was in the back seat," he replied.

"Wait, is Alfred a liar? Is he the type of person that would lie on you? Because if you're being truthful then Alfred is lying. So, who should I believe?"

"Well, I'm telling the truth detective. But what did Alfred lie about?"

"Well, I'm not gonna tell you exactly what he said, because if you both are being honest then your stories should match, right?"

"Yeah," he replied.

"So, I'll ask again, why would Alfred lie on you? Didn't you say y'all were cousins?"

"Yeah, we are, but if you told me what he lied about I can probably straighten it out."

"Alfred said it was just y'all three. Just you, Alfred, and Greg. Is he lying?"

"Yeah. I mean, nah, he right just us three."

"Nobody else was with y'all, just y'all three, right?"

"Nobody else, just us three," he repeated.

"And according to you, Alfred and Greg were in the front seat, while you sat in the back, correct?"

"Yeah, I was in the back seat."

"Then why would he lie and say you and Greg were in the front seat because he told me he was in the backseat."

He begins to hesitate and, "I.. I.. I don't know detective, but I was in the back seat. Maybe he just got it confused or something."

"Well, here's my problem Maurice. I have three people who admit to being present during my case. But they all are pointing the finger at each other. Now in my experience the person who tried to detach themselves from the case completely are usually the ones mostly responsible. Is that you Maurice? Are you the one mostly responsible for this?"

Up to this point Maurice had been looking directly into my eyes, but after my question he became agitated. His voice began to quiver, and uncontrollably shake. "Nooooo detective it wasn't me it was Greg!"

I think to myself, "got him."

"Greg was the one who did this! I was sleep in the car!"

"Okay, okay, okay Maurice, calm down and tell me what happened," I said.

"We were in Greg's car, he was driving. Greg and Alfred were in the front seat and see the white girl. Greg said he was gone get the car. So, we see her park and we parked just to watch her. Somebody pulled up beside her, then pulls right off. So, we waited, and Alfred said what you gone do?

No, wait. I said, man, let's go! Because I'm sleepy, and ready to go to bed. Greg pulls up beside the girl and walks over to her window. He said something to her and comes back to the car. Then we pull off. I thought we were going home, so I dozed off. Next thing I know, I hear a loud POP! We were back by the girl's car, and Greg was out! He ran back over to the car and said, man she tried to run over him. We left the parking lot and went back to Alfred's house."

While listening to suspects talk, I try not to stop them. I believe in allowing them to get their thoughts out. Even if it's not the truth, let them lie! Ultimately, you should have independent evidence to prove otherwise. But in Maurice's statement he did mention information that could be corroborated. One thing he mentioned was that they pulled the car up and spoke with Kayla, which one of my witnesses stated. Also, he said that Greg walked over to the window, which is what Greg admitted to and David verified. But I needed more. "What side of the car did Greg go to?" I asked.

"He went to the driver's side."

"And is that where he shot?"

"Yeah, that's the side he shot," he replied.

"Well how did you see all of that if you were asleep?"

He began to hesitate even more, "But, but, nah man see you trying to trip me up detective."

"No, I'm asking legitimate questions to verify what you're saying. You said you were asleep. But then said you saw something. It can't be both. Either you were asleep, or you saw. I just want you to be truthful, that's all."

We went back and forth for another twenty minutes. He was tired and so was I. I asked, "have you eaten?"

"No, sir," he replied.

"I'm gonna send someone out for some lunch, can I get you something?"

"Yes, Thank you."

I left him in the room with the video recorders still running while I checked up on the progress with the rest of the interviews.

As I exited the interview room the aroma of pizza hit me like a ton of bricks. I'd not eaten yet, so I know my suspects and people we had in custody had not either. Most of them were kids so I asked my team to make sure they ate before continuing with the interviews. My supervisor sprung for the meal so that day everyone ate. Hell, we may have fed defendants that were not on my case.

As we all ate, my team and I talked out my case. We went thru each suspect's statement and witnesses' statements against each one. Greg, by his own admission, he was on the scene. He also admitted that he conspired in the robbery. He also stated that he saw the actual shooting. His statement matches what the independent witness says. So, I know he was there, and he participated in my victim's murder. He's definitely going to jail.

Maurice admits to being on scene of the murder. He admits he waited with Greg as he planned to rob my victim, but becoming tired and went to sleep according to him. His statement is contradicted by the girl's statement.

Both say Maurice was the leader. They also say that Maurice has confessed to them that he was the shooter at one time or another. In that admission, he states exactly how my victim was shot. It's been my experience that the most culpable defendants usually try to place themselves as far as possible from the crime. That's exactly what Maurice was doing. His ass is going to jail!

When I talked about Alfred, his statement seemed he was the least involved. He never admitted to being involved in the planning. The codefendants place him either in the backseat or the passenger side of the vehicle. No one could place him as being the actual person who initially approached the Kayla. After dissecting the case he was present before, during, and after the murder. He was a participant but not as active as the other two.

After talking things out I decided I needed another crack at Alfred. During our conversation he'd left a several pieces of information out. He could provide something else that I missed. Plus, if I could somehow get him to be a witness against the other two, his statement could solidify my case.

I can hear the "charge them all" pundits screaming now. I get that and that's what I wanted. But I had no physical evidence, nor did I have an independent witness that could say who actually did what. So having Alfred testifying as a state's witness could be the glue that holds this case together.

He was there on the scene, he heard the planning, his statement already corroborates what the girls say. Getting him to talking could be key in this case.

As I enter the room, I awake him from sleeping. The room is scattered with leftover pizza crust, drink cans, and napkins. Alfred stretches and yawns, "Detective, can I leave now? Where is my cousin? Are they still here?" he asks.

"Nah man, he's here and a few others are. But most have already left," I replied.

"Alfred, when we talked first you said something that I didn't understand. You said Greg did this, am I correct?"

"Yes sir, Greg did it," he replied.

"Well tell me what happened, and remember, Alfred, I've been talking to people all day. So, if you're gonna be honest, now is the time you should be." I said.

"Greg got out of the car, and he shot her. That's how it happened."

"Well, Alfred you know I'll need details so that answer won't cut it." I'm keeping us both calm this time. No blowups because I want him talking. "Alfred, let's start from when you said, y'all saw her park. What happened after that?"

"I told you, Greg pulled up, walked over to the car, and just shot her. That's what I said the first time!" The inflection in his voice let me know he was blowing up again. So, I try and bring him down.

I calmly responded, "wait a minute, Alfred I need to make sure I understand what you're saying. Just a few minutes ago you said y'all pulled up, Greg got out, and came back to the car. At that point Greg and Maurice began to argue. Is that what happened?"

He loudly replies, "Well, yeah, that's what I said, and Greg shot her!"

I calmly reply, "No, that's not what you said. You never mentioned this time about the parking and watching. I just want to make sure I have your story correct. In order for me to do that I've gotta understand and question the portions that don't make sense."

Now yelling, he says "No, you are trying to confuse me!"

I again calmly reply, "Alfred, the only time a person gets confused during a conversation like this is when they're not being truthful. Up until this point I thought you were being honest with me. What has happened to make that change? If there are points that are missing, then we need to go back over them. In my experience, that's an easy fix if it's the truth. My question now is are you telling me the truth?"

Now crying, he tearfully says, "Man I just wanna go home! Can I just leave?"

I reply, "Alfred we are way beyond that now. I have a young girl dead. Her mother will never see her, kiss her, or touch her again. I also have people saying you are responsible for that. Now you've told me you were there when she died. I just wanna find out what you did. What I do know, is you were there when she died."

"But I didn't do nothing detective," he said.

"Well, if you didn't do anything Alfred, who did?"

Alfred took an extended pause, and said, "Greg, it was Greg. He did it!"

"Okay, Alfred, that's all I was trying to find out. Now tell me how it happened."

He then begins to tell me this elaborate story that begins with, "see me and Maurice were in the back seat and Greg was driving." Now most detectives would stop him right there and call him out on how silly his statement sounded. Sometimes it's almost comical to hear the excuses some suspects will come up with, but as an investigator you must listen. Because within a lie, the truth always lays. So, I've always operated under the guise of, let a suspect lie, and allow the evidence to prove the truth. Nevertheless, I needed more from him.

So, I said, "you didn't think that answer through. Do you really expect me to believe you were chauffeured to a murder?" I kept a straight face while he continued to talk, but I knew where this was going. I was starting to realize that he's not going to confess. While a confession is good, an admission is required. I only needed him to say he was there when Kayla was murdered. I let him continue the lie. He talks for a few more minutes until he ends with, "and Greg got out and shot her."

I asked, "did you see him shoot her?"

"Yes, I saw him shoot her."

"Where in her body did he shoot her?"

"He told me he domed her."

"Domed, what is domed?" I asked.

"He shot her in the head."

"Did he tell you why he shot her?" I asked.

"Man, he wanted the car, but she drove off, so we thought she was still alive."

"So let me ask you this. If Greg got the car, were you supposed to drive his car back to the house?"

"Nooooo man, I wasn't supposed to do nothing!"

"Okay, so it was Maurice then."

"No, man, I didn't say that."

"Well, it had to be one of you guys. If it was Greg's plan to take the car, then he couldn't drive both cars. So, someone had to drive the other car, am I right? My question is, was it you?"

"No, man, I didn't have nothing to do with it, I told you," he said.

"Alfred, I have been working this case for months. You seem to be the one person that's least involved. But your statement is not adding up, and what will eventually happen is you will be grouped in with the person who did pull the trigger. If you are not the trigger man, I don't want you to serve the same time the trigger man will."

Alfred's eyes began to swell as tears gathered underneath them. "I can't do it detective. He is my friend, almost like my family. I won't do my family like that," he said.

"Even if it means spending the rest of your life behind bars?"

"Yeah," he replied as his head dropped into his hands and he began to cry profusely.

It was then that I realized that I had gotten as much information as I could out of Alfred. It was not a confession that I had hoped for, but it was an admission and enough to charge him and everyone involved.

It wasn't uncommon to resolve a case without a confession. In fact, often times, confessions were rare. Gritty police work and the ability to build a case were key. And it was often the job of the prosecutor to create and provide the scenario that led to the crime. My job was to put as much of the elbow grease into the case that I could. In some cases, you won't get a full confession. This case had become so much a part of me that not getting a confession wasn't closure for me. Because the people involved didn't take responsibility for her murder even with the arrests I didn't feel as if Kayla had justice. But justice still was served. It just wasn't as warm as I liked it nor was it as satisfying.

Chapter 11

(Un) Satisfying Ending

I had both Maurice and Alfred transported to jail. Then Rob and I went to Robin's home. I was exhausted. Not from lack of sleep or fatigue, but mentally I was drained. This case had plagued me and Kayla's family for so long and it was finally culminating the way it should have months ago. I felt I owed it to Robin to tell her in person the people responsible for Kayla's murder had been arrested. The drive was quick. One of those drive's where you don't remember anything along the way. I remember leaving the station and I remember arriving. My mind will hold the key to everything I didn't see along the way. As I pulled up to Robin's home, she walked outside to greet us.

We shared pleasantries but I didn't mince words. Robin wouldn't have wanted me to. When I said we had arrested all three suspects in Kayla's case she unleashed a shout of relief and embraced Rob and me. We all shed a tear, and I explained to her that I was unable to obtain confessions, but I was sure all three were the right people. We talked a while longer and I told her there would be another press conference in the morning, but I wouldn't be there.

When cases like Kayla's happen and an arrest is made there is usually a press conference to alert the public. Robin wanted me there and made me promise to attend, which I ended up doing on her behalf. I obtained murder warrants for all three defendants and attended the nighttime press conference with the mayor, my chief of police, FBI director, US marshal, ATF director, my supervisors, Robin, and myself. They all congratulated me on closing Kayla's case. But Robin's speech to the media meant the most. She talked about the sacrifices that had been made by me and my team to close her Kayla's case. She also spoke about how Kayla would not believe how all of this was done for her.

Robin's words meant a lot. But, when she spoke of how she thought the arrest of her child's killers would bring her peace, and it didn't, that was eye opening. It reminded me that every moment in life is precious. Every day away from my children was a day of growth that I missed. Every day away from Anitra was a day I could not show her how much I loved her. And while my job would require me to be away from my family, I needed to learn balance. That following week I did something I had not done since my promotion to homicide. We took a vacation as a family.

Dear Family,

I hope you enjoyed **The Case.** My story is one which I have wanted to tell for years. And it is just in the last year that I have felt comfortable in sitting down to write it out.

As an author, I love to receive feedback. You are the reason I write, and I want to hear what you enjoyed about this book, what you loved, and yes, even the critical feedback.

I would like to ask you a favor. If so inclined, I'd love a review of **The Case**. Loved it, or if you didn't —I would simply enjoy your feedback.

Reviews for a writer are what allow us to not only promote our books but also give us insight into what you, as the reader are looking for when you purchase a book. The reader wields the power to make or break a book. I would appreciate if you took a few moments of your time to provide a book review on Amazon, Goodreads, or wherever else my books may be sold.

Thank you so much for reading **The Case** and for spending your time with me.

Your friend,

Christopher

Made in the USA
Columbia, SC
18 March 2024

32981051R00098